Rethinking Rights

Rethinking Rights

Historical Development and Philosophical Justification

Eleanor Curran

LEXINGTON BOOKS

Lanham • Boulder • New York • London

Published by Lexington Books
An imprint of The Rowman & Littlefield Publishing Group, Inc.
4501 Forbes Boulevard, Suite 200, Lanham, Maryland 20706
www.rowman.com

86–90 Paul Street, London EC2A 4NE

Ch. 3 reprinted: This chapter, from the second paragraph onwards, was first published as "An Immodest Proposal: Hobbes Rather than Locke Provides a Forerunner for Modern rights Theory" in *Law and Philosophy*, Vol. 32, No. 4 (July 2013): 515–38, Springer Nature.

British Library Cataloguing in Publication Information Available

Library of Congress Cataloging-in-Publication Data

Names: Curran, Eleanor, 1956- author.
Title: Rethinking rights : historical development and philosophical justification / Eleanor Curran.
Other titles: Rethinking rights
Description: Lanham, Maryland : Lexington Books, [2022] | Includes bibliographical references and index.
Identifiers: LCCN 2022003954 (print) | LCCN 2022003955 (ebook) | ISBN 9781498547871 (Cloth) | ISBN 9781498547895 (paperback) | ISBN 9781498547888 (eBook)
Subjects: LCSH: Human rights. | Civil rights. | Law—Philosophy. | Law and ethics.
Classification: LCC JC571 .C84 2022 (print) | LCC JC571 (ebook) | DDC 323—dc23/ eng/20220304
LC record available at https://lccn.loc.gov/2022003954
LC ebook record available at https://lccn.loc.gov/2022003955

For Deborah

Contents

Acknowledgements

I would like to thank Quentin Skinner, Sharon Lloyd, and Larry May for writing in support of this project in its early stages, when I still thought that my examination of the history of rights theorising would lead me to a neo-Hobbesian theory of Rights. I would like to thank Quentin Skinner again and Philip Pettit for helping to convince me, by their work on "Republican Liberty," that Hobbes's notion of liberty is inadequate for a modern theory of rights. I am very grateful to the late Brian Tierney for his wonderful work and scholarship excavating the history of the idea of natural rights. I would also like to thank Emily Haslam for her kind and helpful comments on chapter 6 and I am grateful to an anonymous reviewer for Lexington Books for very helpful comments and suggestions.

My thanks to Toni Williams for allowing me to reduce my teaching at Kent Law School during a crucial period in 2019/2020. I am grateful to Louisa Millen for research assistance early on and to Raul Madden for research assistance in the final stages and especially for going the extra mile as I was coming up to my deadline.

My thanks to Davina Cooper and Edward Kanterian for encouragement and support.

The book owes much to the students on my Morality and Law course which traced the history of the idea of individual rights and of the philosophical assessment of rights. Their questions and comments kept me focussed on how rights are understood and why they matter.

Finally, I am very grateful to Jana Hodges-Klück, senior acquisitions editor at Lexington Books and also to Sydney Wedbush, for their patience and unfailing courteousness and encouragement.

Introduction

"All people have certain rights simply by virtue of their humanity; these rights are inviolable and should be respected and protected." This idea of *natural rights* developed gradually through the late medieval and into the early modern period, as the notion of *ius* (right) changed in its meaning from objective right to subjective right. It became a particularly powerful concept in political philosophy, inspiring much of modern liberal political theory. And while the idea of *universal individual rights* has continued to grow in strength and influence (and is now prevalent in the guise of *human rights* and within international and domestic law as well as in international political discourse), its philosophical justification has had a much more uneven history.

The development of the notion of subjective rights, attached to all individuals, was the subject of much philosophical work and some of the resulting theories of natural rights provided strong philosophical justifications for individual rights. They usually started from theological premises such as that God created us as equals and moving from that (e.g. in Locke) to the establishment of equal rights not to be attacked and invaded. They also usually relied on the notion of natural law, known by all rational beings, which allows the Spanish scholastic Las Casas, for example, to argue that liberty is a right instilled in each of us by our rational nature, that is, from natural law. These early theories of natural rights had the advantages of an unassailable moral authority and an objective moral law to appeal to as part of the justification of the rights. The best of these arguments were powerful and persuasive, as long as their premises were accepted as true.

The philosophical justifications of natural rights met their demise, however, with the attacks of David Hume and Jeremy Bentham in the eighteenth century. Hume's criticism that natural law theory made a logical mistake when it derived moral conclusions from factual premises was seen as devastating. At a more general level, philosophical justifications that relied on theological and metaphysical premises could not survive the criticisms of the new empiricists and legal positivists. The philosophical credibility of theories of natural rights and natural law were irreparably damaged in the eyes of all but a few (mostly Catholic) philosophers. This left a large theoretical hole to fill if the notion of individual rights was to survive with any philosophical respectability. The book is, in part, an examination of the history of the idea of individual rights and how that history has been written by those seeking to find philosophical explanations and justifications of rights.

The book also grew out of questions that my first book left unanswered. After examining Hobbes's extraordinary pronouncements on subjects' rights in *Leviathan,* I searched for a theory of rights that I could fit Hobbes into. I gradually realised that while he doesn't propose a theory of *natural rights* in the *natural law tradition* of Locke and others, neither does he conform in a satisfactory way, to any of the modern, secular theories of rights that replaced those theories. I found that the Hohfeldian analysis of legal rights, now so widely used by rights theorists, could not accurately capture Hobbesian subjects' rights, despite the arguments of some Hobbes scholars, that all subjects' rights are Hohfeldian *liberty rights*. This has led, in my view, to a distorted reading of Hobbes's theory of rights that sees subjects' rights as being weak and ineffectual.

My search for a suitable theoretical home for Hobbesian rights led to a realization that the domination of modern rights theorising by the Hohfeldian analysis in particular and the jurisprudential study of rights in general, was worth closer examination, as it had taken rights theorising in a different direction from natural rights theory. While natural rights theory, which first explored the notion that all humans have certain rights, focussed on the moral and political values and reasoning attached to that idea, modern, jurisprudential rights theorising is more focussed on a careful conceptual analysis of all rights, and especially of legal rights.

I was struck by the stark contrast between the beginning of conceptualizing and theorising individual rights in theories of *natural rights*, and modern theorising of rights which has emerged largely from analytical jurisprudence in the twentieth century. There is a puzzling disconnect between the early philosophical exploration of the idea that all people have certain rights, and twentieth and early twenty-first century philosophical work on rights. The former is concerned with the big questions of moral and political philosophy, while the latter generally concerns itself with the rigorous analysis of the concept of a right and, sometimes, but not always, with its justification.

The rejection of the theological and metaphysical premises of natural rights theory led to a jurisprudential turn in rights theorising and while commentators often briefly acknowledge the origins of the notion of individual rights in natural rights theory, they usually then ignore that history in their subsequent explorations of the concept of rights. I think this has been a case of throwing the baby out with the bath water and that the history of such an important idea is worth re-examining. The detailed task of digging out that history and putting it together has of course been done in the superb work of Brian Tierney and others, but what I have tried to do here is to re-visit a little of that history in order to examine the effect of its rejection on subsequent rights theorising.

The aim of the book is to examine the history of rights theory and the effects of that history and how it has been written, on how philosophers think about rights today, including how they assess historical writing on rights. This leads to a re-examination of some commentary on historical writers on rights, which in turn leads to a critical examination of the enormous influence of the Hohfeldian analysis of legal rights on modern philosophy of rights. While Hohfeld does have his critics, I think it is fair to say that modern rights theorising is largely Hohfeldian, both in its acceptance of the Hohfeldian categories of rights, and of the Hohfeldian *claim right* as an exemplar of a moral or political right as well as a legal right.

I argue that the dominance of the Hohfeldian analysis in rights theorising leads to some limitations when the analysis is applied to the study of moral and political rights. The first part of the critique of the use of the Hohfeldian analysis in rights theorising, concerns its use to interpret historical writing on rights. In chapter 5, I look at some of the commentary on Locke's and Hobbes's contributions to rights theory and argue that by superimposing Hohfeldian categories on the work of these historical figures, we get distorted readings of their contributions to rights theory. In chapter 6, I develop a more general critique of the Hohfeldian approach to rights, when it is applied to moral and political rights. I argue that a Hohfeldian approach imposes some particular restrictions on theorists and also that the notion of the *claim right* is itself lacking in all content and cannot be connected to any moral or political value that might support or justify it as an important concept, apart from its correlative relationship to the duties of others.

The only area of rights theorising that is often less in thrall to Hohfeld, is that of recent work on *human rights* and so I also look briefly at human rights theorising in chapter 7. The philosophy of human rights is interesting in that it marks, to some extent, a return to the subject matter of natural rights. Like natural rights theory, its focus is on universal moral and political rights that attach to humans simply by virtue of their humanity. In seeking to justify human rights these writers often argue for a particular grounding concept for rights, such as human agency or human need. A closer look reveals that attempts to find a grounding concept often end by moving to multiple grounding concepts.

As well as Hohfeld's legal analysis, there are also more conventional *theories of rights*, the two most important modern theories being the will and interest theories. There is an ongoing debate about which theory succeeds but as both suffer from counterexamples, they both, in a certain sense, fail to explain what a right is. I briefly address the impasse in the ongoing debates between the will and interest theories in chapter 7.

Finally, I make some tentative suggestions for future rights theorising in an attempt to solve some of the problems I have drawn attention to in previous chapters. In particular, I suggest an alternative to the Hohfeldian *claim right* that replaces the Hohfeldian notion of a (legal) claim with that of a "justified claim" using the older idea of "staking a claim" in the sense of saying "this is mine" or "this should be mine." This introduces moral content or value, to the notion of a claim, that I have argued is missing from the Hohfeldian claim. I also suggest four distinct categories of rights, three of which arise from different aspects of human nature and describe various kinds of individual rights. The fourth, "rights of (legal/social) organisation," includes those more technical legal rights that apply to specific individuals or groups or other legal entities, not because of their human nature or moral status but because of their legal status. This fourth category is different to the other three and does not come under the heading of "individual rights." My intention is to distinguish these kinds of legal rights as a distinct category of rights, which only attach to those with a particular legal status and are therefore importantly different from *universal moral and political rights*. It is these universal moral and political rights that were first conceived as *natural rights* and are now often termed *human rights*, and which need to be explained and justified in quite different ways from the technical legal rights that they have been associated with since the jurisprudential turn in rights theorising.

The last chapter is both tentative and speculative and only time and a great deal more work will show whether the suggestions for future rights theorising have something to contribute to ongoing debates. The rest of the book, that is, chapters 1–7, should stand independently and not be colored by the speculative nature of my proposals in chapter 8. The arguments of chapters 1–7, concerning the history of rights theory and the shortcomings of some of its developments, which affect rights theorising to the present day, will, I hope, be taken on their own merits.

Part I

THE HISTORY OF RIGHTS THEORY

Chapter 1

The Beginning

The Rise of the Idea of Natural Rights

THE BACKGROUND

The idea that people have rights cannot be traced to a precise date or to a particular author or piece of writing. It is a matter of debate when, precisely, the notion that we have rights to certain things or to particular freedoms, first emerged, though it is thought to fall somewhere between the twelfth and the early sixteenth centuries. There is general agreement, however, on the fact that there was no genuinely comparable notion in either ancient Rome or ancient Greece; so, we can say when political philosophy *lacked* the idea of subjective individual rights. When and how exactly it gained such a notion is more contested and more complex. In terms of language, it is to the words *ius* (usually translated as "right" but also sometimes translated as "law" or "justice") and *dominium* (usually translated as "property") that we should turn our attention, in trying to trace the gradual change from the notion of objective right to subjective right.[1] In terms of theoretical underpinning, there is extensive (though not universal) agreement that theories of natural rights attach to theories of natural law. Although the notion of subjective rights for all individuals is not found in ancient Greek or ancient Roman writing, ideas of natural law are of course present from the Stoics onwards and provide a continuity of thinking on the existence of a universal, objective moral law, known by reason and governing all peoples and all places. In the writings of the Christian philosophers of the early modern period these two ideas come together in theories of natural rights that come to dominate political theory and practice in the seventeenth and eighteenth centuries, fuelling arguments on the Parliamentarian side in the English Civil War and culminating in the justifications for the American and French revolutions.

The Subjective Turn

The phrase *ius naturale* or "natural right" was originally used to refer to what is naturally just or right, that is, what is just or right according to natural law. This is the objective use of the term. But over time there was a change in meaning from the notion of what is right according to natural law, to a natural right that an individual has to something. The change is from what is naturally right for person X, to person X's natural right to something. It is a change from an objective notion of what is right, dictated by natural law and applied to an individual, to a subjective right located *in the individual* rather than in objective law. Now the term *ius* or "right" is being used in quite a different way. We can now say that *person X has a right to Y* rather than *it is right that person X has Y*. There are various ways this new meaning can be understood—as a liberty or a faculty or a power of the individual. But the important change to be noted first is from the objective to the subjective use of the term right.[2] Another way to put it, is as a change from "what natural law dictates is right," to "what the individual claims by right for herself."

Some of the most significant work on tracing the subjective turn in the meaning of *ius* is in the writing of Michel Villey. Villey is the first of the modern scholars to contrast *natural rights* with the older natural right in the sense of what is objectively right or just according to natural law. He argues that it is in the work of the scholastic philosopher William of Ockham, in the early fourteenth century, that the subjective meaning is first given to *ius* and that instead of objective right it refers to a faculty, ability, liberty, or power to act. It is in the context of Ockham's nominalist philosophy, according to which only individuals have real existence, that this stress on the individual can be understood and brought to bear on political philosophy.[3]

Ius and *Dominium*—Active and Passive Rights

From the early days of the new subjective meaning given to the terms *ius* and *dominium* there is a distinction to be drawn between two ways of understanding the nature of a right. This distinction is still with us today and is usually expressed as the distinction between "active" and "passive" rights. It is illustrated by a quotation from Dominican theologian Silvestro Mazzolinida Prierio, from 1515, quoted by Richard Tuck at the start of the first chapter of his important book on the history of natural rights theories.

> *Dominium,* according to some people, is the same thing as *ius.* So that anyone who has a *ius* in something, has *dominium* over it; and anyone who has a *ius* to the use of something, has dominium in it, and vice versa. . . . According to other people, it is not identical, for an inferior does not have *dominium* over a

superior, but he may have a *ius* against him. Thus for example, a son has a *ius* to be fed by his father, and the member of a congregation has a *ius* to receive the sacrament from a prelate, etc. So they say, to have *dominium* implies that one has a *ius*, but not vice versa; for in addition to a *ius* one must have superiority.[4]

We can see from this passage the seeds of the discussion about whether rights are active, implying a power or control or a choice on the part of the right holder, or passive and requiring recognition and/or protection or provision by others. The distinction is important for Tuck as it is at the centre of his argument that some early theories of natural rights, including those of Grotius and Hobbes, are distinctive for describing "active" rights and that this can be traced back to the emergence of a theory in the fifteenth century that defined a natural right as a faculty or power which in turn allowed the move to the notion of a natural right as a liberty.

So far then, we have the new notion of a subjective right, a right that is attached to the person; a right which states what that person may claim in terms of the duties of others towards them or what they are free to do or have a power to do. The theoretical or philosophical context for morality at this time is of course natural law theory, which, as mentioned above, had been present in moral thinking from the Stoics through ancient Greece and ancient Rome but at this stage is in its Christian medieval form (particularly represented by Aquinas), and that of the early modern period.

THE RELATIONSHIP OF EARLY NATURAL RIGHTS THEORIES TO NATURAL LAW

It is generally accepted that early and classical theories of natural rights attach to theories of natural law. This is not to say that the relationship is straightforward or simple or that the view that natural rights theories grew out of natural law theory does not have its detractors. The most common view is that natural rights theories emerged from natural law, or at least from natural law thinking, and are therefore a part of that tradition. Further, they may be said to be dependent upon theories of natural law or dependent upon natural law premises. For example, in the introduction to *Philosophical Foundations of Human Rights*, the authors say that the "idea of rights held by all in virtue of their humanity" can be found "[i]n the guise of 'natural rights'—rights held by people as a matter of natural law—," and that this idea is "found in the influential seventeenth and eighteenth century work of Grotius, Pufendorf, Locke, and Kant."[5]

Natural law theory dominated thinking on morality during the period when the idea of natural rights developed, so it is hardly surprising that

there is a close connection between the two and that most of those writing on natural rights were doing so in the context of natural law theory.
Many of the major advocates of natural rights theory such as Grotius,
Pufendorf and Locke, developed their theories of natural rights as part of
their works on natural law. Locke's theory of natural rights, for example,
is developed within his political theory which is explicitly dependent on
natural law theory.

> The *state of nature* has a law of nature to govern it, which obliges every one:
> and reason, which is that law, teaches all mankind, who will but consult it, that
> being all *equal* and *independent,* no one ought to harm another in his life, health,
> liberty, or possessions: for men being all the workmanship of one omnipotent,
> and infinitely wise maker; all the servants of one sovereign master, sent into
> the world by his order, and about his business; they are his property, whose
> workmanship they are, made to last during his, not one another's pleasure: and
> being furnished with like faculties, sharing all in one community of nature, there
> cannot be supposed any such *subordination* among us, that may authorize us to
> destroy one another, as if we were made for one another's uses, as the inferior
> ranks of creatures are for our's.[6]

This passage makes clear the extent to which Locke's theory is one of
traditional natural law and the way in which the natural law premises from
Christian theology form the basis of the argument for natural rights. The
next part of the passage moves to the notion that all humans have natural
rights.

> Every one, as he is *bound to preserve himself,* and not to quit his station wil-
> fully, so by the like reason, when his own preservation comes not in competi-
> tion, ought he, as much as he can, to *preserve the rest of mankind,* and may not,
> unless it be to do justice on an offender, take away, or impair the life, or what
> tends to the preservation of life, the liberty, health, limb or goods of another.
>   And that all men may be restrained from invading others rights.[7]

I quote this passage at length because it provides a clear illustration of how
classical ideas of natural rights are usually connected to and dependent upon
the natural law theories of the medieval and early modern philosophers. It
also illustrates the influence of Christian theology on both theories of natural
law and of natural rights. The pathway that has been perceived to lead from
early theories of natural rights, like that of Locke, to modern liberal theories
of rights, is not as straightforward as one might think, however. I will briefly
outline below some of the reasons for this and in chapter 3 I will argue for an
alternative route to modern theories of rights via Hobbes rather than Locke.

CONFLICTING VIEWS OF THE RELATIONSHIP
BETWEEN NATURAL RIGHTS AND NATURAL LAW

The history of the relationship of natural rights to natural law that is often assumed is the apparently straightforward one above. But there are other, conflicting views of this relationship and of the implications for theories of natural rights. One such view goes back to Michel Villey and his observation that the meaning of *ius* had changed from one of objective right to subjective right. Characterising the new understanding of subjective right as a "power" to act on the part of the individual, Villey points out that *ius,* understood as objective and dictated by law could not be the same as *ius* understood as a liberty or faculty or power to act. In fact, given that law is a restraint on action they must be in some way contradictory or as Tierney puts it "the two concepts were antithetical, radically incompatible with one another."[8] In other words, an *ius* or "right" cannot be at the same time, a freedom or power to act and a *restraint on action.* If we accept this argument, then it is hard to see how we can accept the view that natural rights theories come from or are dependent on natural law theories.

Leo Strauss makes a similar point which he expresses in a famous remark about Hobbes. "Hobbes obviously starts, not, as the great tradition did, from natural 'law,' that is, from an objective order, but from natural 'right,' that is, from an absolutely justified subjective claim which, far from being dependent on any previous law, order, or obligation, is itself the origin of all law, order, or obligation."[9] The shift is a crucial one for Strauss, marking a move from the authority of natural law to the justified claims asserted by individuals.

This discussion, of the relationship of natural rights theory to natural law theory, takes us back to the question of whether matters of objective right expressed in natural law can possibly give rise to claims of subjective rights, particularly when those rights are conceived as liberties. Hobbes is an example of a philosopher who defines rights as liberties[10] and who argues that rights are the opposite of laws even though they have been confused with law in the past.

> . . . they that speak of this subject, use to confound *Jus,* and *Lex, Right* and *Law;* yet they ought to be distinguished; because RIGHT, consisteth in liberty to do, or to forebeare; Whereas Law, determineth, and bindeth to one of them: so that Law, and Right, differ as much, as Obligation and Liberty; which in one and the same matter are inconsistent.[11]

In *De Cive* Hobbes makes the point even more pithily, "a *law* is a *bond*, a *right* is a *liberty*, and they differ as contraries."[12]

We can see the argument here, that we cannot derive a freedom or liberty from an obligation or law. Indeed, as Hobbes says, they are surely opposites or contraries. Either you are obligated to do something, or you are free to do it. And yet, when we see subjective rights, say, as liberties, we can also see the rights as liberties which we *should* have or which *should* be respected or protected. Now the question arises "according to what law or principle should we have such rights?" Immediately we see that we can go back once more to principles of natural law. I will argue in chapter 3 that Hobbes does not appeal to traditional natural law principles to justify his theory of rights and this is what makes his theory uniquely modern, but many early natural rights theorists *do* appeal directly to principles of natural law.

It is worth noting that Tierney argues against the notion that natural rights conceived as part of natural law are incompatible with natural rights conceived as subjective rights. He argues, against Villey, that "the various senses of *ius* he discusses are not contradictory concepts. Rather they are correlative."[13] In affirming a "right ordering of human relationships" he says we "imply a structure of rights and duties" and can emphasise either the rights or the duties. "The resulting works may be very different in tone and spirit, but the different emphases do not necessarily imply logical contradictions."[14] In addition, and perhaps even more interestingly, he also draws attention to another aspect of the traditional natural law teaching of the canonists, which is that as well as providing commands and prohibitions on the actions of individuals, natural law sometimes defines "an area of permissiveness where agents were free to act as they chose."[15] This notion of "permissive natural law" allows for natural rights to be understood as liberties and powers to act which individuals are designated to hold *within the boundaries* of natural law.

I will leave these arguments for now as the purpose of this chapter is to trace the early history of the notion of individual rights as it has been written, rather than to engage in detailed argument about whether or not particular interpretations and analyses are justified. That will be left for later chapters. Regarding the relationship of natural rights to natural law, the view that dominates commentary is that natural rights do come out of natural law theory and are to some extent dependent upon it. For now, it is important to draw out what is distinctive in the new understanding of natural rights as subjective rights.

WHAT IS NEW AND SIGNIFICANT IN THE NOTION OF "NATURAL RIGHTS?"

So far in this chapter, I have sketched the historical and philosophical context of the emerging notion of natural rights. In the next part of the chapter, I will provide some more detail of the development of the idea of natural rights in discussions of the theories of Grotius and Locke and I will show how the notion of natural rights was used by both sides in the political debates of the English Civil War. But before that I want to pause and consider what is original and significant in the new idea of natural rights. The first and most obvious thing, as I have already discussed, is the change from an objective understanding of *ius* or "right" to a subjective understanding. This moves the moral focus from natural *law*, which exists outside those it commands, and sets out what is morally right (and wrong) for all, to the individual and what she may claim as her moral *right* to certain freedoms or to have certain things or to make certain choices. And while this changes the *focus* of our moral thinking, it usually remains within the orbit of natural law in as much as natural law influences or even dictates which rights we can be said to have.

What might we say is new in the idea of natural rights? Natural rights are universal, they apply to all people. This seems unsurprising perhaps, in the context of natural law, which is also universal in its application. But it is very surprising in the context of other existing notions of what we can call "rights." So, we might talk of the rights of kings or the rights of trustees or the rights of members of guilds. These sorts of legal and social rights apply to specific individuals or groups under particular legal or social rules. The rights are held because of the status or role of the person or group and are dependent upon that status or role. So, for example, a person who is a member of a guild might have certain rights (and duties) according to the rules of the guild and if they were no longer a member of the guild such rights (and duties) would no longer apply. In the case of legal rights, these rights are held under particular laws and if the laws change then the rights can also change or even cease to exist. Natural rights are distinct from these other kinds of rights in as much as they are not dependent on any specific rules or laws. If one has a natural right to X, that right exists (as a moral right) whether or not it exists in law. The natural right to X is inviolable as well as universal.

An argument could be made against the significance of the distinction I am drawing. One could say that with natural rights one does no more than *extend* the role or status, to which the rights apply, to all humans. This is still a category and excludes, for example, all other animals. This argument carries some weight, particularly when one thinks of current debates regarding animal rights, but there is a reply available to me. I can argue that there is still something new and significant in the notion that certain rights apply to all humans regardless of either personal circumstances or laws or rules specific to a group or a society. What is new is the moral and political significance of claiming that natural rights apply to all and cannot be abrogated by any human laws. This universality, as I have said, ties into the universality of natural law and historically this has usually tied into notions of a moral law that exists outside and beyond human beings with an objective existence and the super-human, unassailable moral authority of God. In early discussions of natural rights, which are usually applying natural law principles, the same universality applies. So, at least in this historical context, there is still a strong argument that natural rights are significantly different from previous legal and social rights.

There is another reason why natural rights represent a new and significant way of thinking about rights and that is the moral principle that is required before one could conceive of natural rights. This is the principle of the equal moral worth of all human beings, regardless of their circumstances. Such a principle sounds commonplace now of course, but it is worth remembering that in the period we are discussing and before, in ancient Greece and Rome, for example, there was no such principle. Indeed, the opposite was the case. The prevailing belief was of a natural hierarchy amongst humans, according to which, some were fit to rule and others to be ruled.

From the twelfth to the early sixteenth centuries, canonists and scholastics debated the new subjective meaning of *ius naturale* and its many implications. But, as Tierney points out, these scholarly debates took place against a background of established rights of various groups in relation to one another. As Tierney puts it,

> Feudal society was a structure of interlocking rights—the rights of lords and vassals in relation to one another. And within feudal society many new communal associations were growing up that claimed specific rights and liberties for their members—city communes and innumerable guilds of merchants and craftsmen. This widespread concern for rights is famously exemplified in the Anglo-American tradition by our cherished Magna Carta . . . the document went on to specify various rights of feudal lords and vassals and of merchants and sometimes of all free Englishmen.[16]

Here we can see that even "all free Englishmen" names a particular group of people. My intention is to pick out the elements of this record that are directly relevant to those rights whose history I am trying to trace, that is, the history of *natural rights* or, to use a more theoretically neutral phrase, *individual rights*.

Part of the purpose of this book, is to differentiate the notion of *individual rights* (now often expressed as "human rights"), from the more generic legal, political, and social rights of different groups and persons with a particular status or role. The rights and duties of such actors in relation to one another were being debated and legislated during the same era and were nothing new at that time. Indeed, we could trace the history of those rights back to ancient Greece and Rome and beyond. If we were to refer to a king's rights or a nobleman's rights or even to parliament's rights as "human rights" it would immediately be clear that we were making an error in mixing up these two kinds of rights. Indeed, the older understanding of a right as something due to someone because of their role or status can be found in the Roman jurists and so harps back to the objective use of *ius*. To give someone their right in this sense is to give them their due, in other words what is due to them according to legal or political arrangements of the time. Tierney refers to Villey's colourful illustration of this point. The Roman use of *ius* "refers to the just share, the just due, of someone within an established structure of social relationships, varying with each person's status and role. In this sense the word *ius* could imply a disadvantage to an individual. Villey observes that the *ius* of parricide was to be sewn up in a sack of vipers and thrown into the Tiber."[17]

EXAMPLES FROM EARLY WRITING
ON NATURAL RIGHTS

One example of a new and distinct *natural right* is the right of all individuals to defend themselves in a court of law against charges brought against them. This was argued by jurists in the thirteenth century to be a natural right similar to that of a right to defend ourselves against physical assault.

> Towards the end of the [thirteenth] century jurists began to argue that the right to appear and defend oneself before a court of law—what we should call a right to due process—was not just a part of the civil law of particular nations but rather was grounded in the universal natural law. They argued that, just as there was a natural right of self-defence against physical assault, so too should there be a right to defend oneself against legal charges.[18]

This idea of the universality of natural law is particularly well expressed by Cicero.

> True law is right reason in agreement with nature; it is of universal application, unchanging and everlasting; it summons to duty by its commands, and averts from wrongdoing by its prohibitions. And it does not lay its commands or prohibitions upon good men in vain, though neither have any effect on the wicked. It is a sin to try to alter this law, nor is it allowable to attempt to repeal any part of it, and it is impossible to abolish it entirely. We cannot be freed from its obligations by senate or people, and we need to look outside ourselves for an expounder or interpreter of it. And there will not be different laws at Rome or Athens, or different laws now and in the future, but one eternal and

unchangeable law will be valid for all nations and all times, and there will be one master and ruler, that is, God, over us all, for he is the author of this law, its promulgator, and its enforcing judge.[19]

At the other end of the period of innovation in rights language and of the developing idea of natural rights, there are the arguments of the Spanish Dominican, Las Casas who, after living among the conquered American Indians for twenty years, and then studying theology and law, defended the rights of the American Indians against their Spanish conquerors.[20] The natural rights the Indians were said to have by Las Casas, included those to liberty, to own property, to self-defence, and to form their own governments. The natural right to liberty is particularly important here with Las Casas arguing that it applied to each individual Indian such that even if the majority of Indians consented to be ruled by the Spanish, the rights of minority dissenters must be respected.[21]

Another remark from Las Casas illustrates an important feature that marks out natural rights in the new subjective sense from previous meanings. He says that ". . . liberty is a right (*ius*) necessarily instilled in man from the beginning of rational nature and so from natural law (*iure*)."[22] This is a right that attaches to individuals prior to any rights that arise out of relationships within an organized society, prior, in other words, to any particular law or political arrangements. Natural rights are rights that are universal and attached to all individuals, as a matter of moral principle, derived from objective natural law.

Las Casas wrote extensively and argued passionately in defence of the rights of the American Indians and particularly their right to natural liberty. There is some controversy regarding the interpretation of his writing and whether the right to liberty he refers to really represents new thinking on subjective rights or is rather an application of traditional Thomist natural law. Tierney argues, convincingly in my view, that it is the former. He argues that Las Casas used a combination of ancient and medieval texts of political and moral theory along with many references to legal texts. For example, in what Tierney calls a "crucial definition of liberty" (as mentioned above) in his later work, *De Regia Potestate*, Las Casas interweaves "Thomist and juristic texts" to say the following,

As regards humans, it is shown that from the beginning of their rational nature, they were born free, as in the law Manumissiones of the Digest, . . . The reason for this according to Thomas . . . is that a rational nature in itself is not ordered to some other as its end. . . . For liberty is a right (ius) necessarily instilled in man from the beginning of rational nature and so from natural law (iure) as in Distinctio 1 (of the Decretum) . . .[23]

Las Casas used his reading of law and of Aquinas to develop arguments defending the American Indians in terms of their subjective rights. He "defended the Indians' right to liberty and their correlative right to consent to Spanish rule."[24] Furthermore, applying a rule of cannon law concerning the right to consent of "all whom the matter touches"[25] combined with another cannon law rule that "a group of persons could possess a right either as a corporate whole or as single individuals."[26] Las Casas argued that even the consent of a whole people or city could not take away the right of a single individual to withhold consent. As Tierney puts it "this amounted to a very extreme defence of the individual right to liberty."[27] And it illustrates very nicely, the difference between the new *natural rights* and traditional legal and social rights.

Tierney also makes the point that regardless of how eccentric it may have been to combine Thomistic and juridical arguments in this way, to justify claims of individual rights, the Spanish Dominicans "needed a doctrine of natural rights, above all to cope with the moral problems raised by the Spanish Conquests in America." And one consequence of these arguments was that "when new problems arose in the early modern era, a theory of natural rights was widely diffused and was readily available for use by future generations of jurists and philosophers."[28]

In conclusion, one can see that in terms of the moral principles of equality and the equal worth of all humans and the universality of natural rights that these principles engender, we are discussing rights of a quite different kind from those that would include the rights of feudal lords and the rights of trustees. A further question that arises for the philosophy of rights, however, is whether, having distinguished these different types of rights (or some might say, rights with a different extension), they can be brought back together again via a rigorous conceptual analysis of the term "right" (or a focus on intension). We might express this question by adapting the political slogan to ask, "is there more that unites different kinds of rights than that which divides them?" This question will be addressed later in the book but for now there is much more to be said about the historical development of theories of rights and how that history has been written.

CLASSICAL NATURAL RIGHTS
THEORY—HUGO GROTIUS

Hugo Grotius is generally accepted as an important figure in the development of the early modern version of natural law and natural rights theory. He makes (at least) two significant moves regarding natural law. First, he puts man's natural sociability as a source of natural law and second, he famously says that even if God did not exist, natural law would still be true.[29] This latter point is significant as it demonstrates that while most natural law theory relies on theological premises, it is possible to make an argument for natural law on non-theological premises. An important example of this is John Finnis's modern theory of natural law and natural rights, which is written without theological premises.[30] It is important, however, not to overstate the case for the "secularism" of Grotius's theory, as it remains a theory with important connections to theological principles, despite the famous remarks regarding the logical strength of the theory, even without the premise of God's existence. The notion of human beings' innate sociability, for example, as well as that of universal human access to reason, both stem from a belief that we are created in God's image.[31] And, right after making the point that the logic of natural law cannot be altered even by God, he reminds us that God "is the sovereign Lord of our lives and of all things."[32] Indeed, Tierney argues, along these lines, that the view that Grotius represents a "modern, secular" approach to natural rights and natural law is mistaken; pointing out that after the famous "impious hypothesis" Grotius added "that there was indeed a God and that God's free will was 'another source of law besides the source in nature.'"[33]

Grotius on Rights

Grotius uses the term "right" in both the old objective sense and the new subjective sense. He says, at the beginning of *De Iure Belli ac Pacis,* that "right signifies nothing more than what is just, and that, more in a negative than a positive sense; so that RIGHT is that which is not unjust." He goes on, "[n] ow any thing is unjust, which is repugnant to the nature of society, established among rational creatures."[34] In other words, anything which goes against natural law is unjust. "Natural right is the dictate of right reason, shewing the moral turpitude, or moral necessity, of any act from its agreement or disagreement with a rational nature, and consequently that such an act is either forbidden or commanded by God, the author of that nature."[35] So, he is using "right" in the old objective sense of what is just as dictated by natural law. But he also refers to the subjective use of "right." "There is another Signification of the word RIGHT . . . which relates directly to the person. In which sense, RIGHT is a moral quality annexed to the person, justly entitling him to possess some particular privilege, or to perform some particular act. . . ."[36] Grotius then refers to rights which are connected to things. "This right is annexed to the person, although it sometimes follows the things, as the services of lands, which are called REAL RIGHTS, in opposition to those merely PERSONAL. Not because these rights are not annexed to persons, but the distinction is made, because they belong to the persons only who possess some particular things." So, now he is referring to rights held because of a particular status or role occupied by a person, in this example, as a property owner. He goes on, "This moral Quality when perfect, is called by us a *Faculty;* when imperfect, an *Aptitude:* The former answers to the *Act*, and the latter to the *Power*, when we speak of natural Things."[37] Grotius carries on referring to both these sorts of rights. "Civilians call a faculty that Right, which every man has to his own; but we shall hereafter, taking it in its strict and proper sense, call it a right. This right comprehends the power, that we have over ourselves, which is called liberty, and the power, that we have over others, as that of a father over his children, and of a master over his slaves."[38]

Grotius is putting the two kinds of rights side by side and discussing them as two examples of rights that may be distinguished from each other yet are both attached to the person, so both are subjective rights. We might say that Grotius's theory marks a point just before we find fully fledged natural rights theory which jettisons both the old objective understanding of "right" and those rights that are attached to a particular role or status, leaving only what we might term "pure natural rights" or moral and political natural rights, which are universal, attaching to each human being regardless of any role or status they may occupy. Grotius moves from the principle of man's innate sociability to the duty to respect the rights of others.

This Sociability, . . . or this Care of maintaining Society in a Manner conformable to the Light of human Understanding, is the Fountain of Right, properly so called; to which belongs the Abstaining from that which is another's, and the Restitution of what we have of another's, or of the Profit we have made by it, the Obligation of fulfilling Promises, the Reparation of a Damage done through our own Default, and the Merit of Punishment among Men.[39]

He also links the moral duty to respect the rights of others with natural law. "Right Reason, and the Nature of Society, . . . does not prohibit all Manner of Violence, but only that which is repugnant to Society, that is, which invades another's Right: for the Design of Society is, that everyone should quietly enjoy his own, with the Help, and by the united Force of the whole Community."[40] And he also says,

as there is one kind of social tie founded upon an equality, for instance, among brothers, citizens, friends, allies, and another on pre-eminence, as Aristotle styles it, subsisting between parents and children, masters and servants, sovereigns and subjects, God and men. So justice takes place either amongst equals, or between the governing and the governed parties, notwithstanding their difference of rank. The former of these, if I am not mistaken, may be called the right of equality, and the latter the right of superiority.[41]

Once again, Grotius is putting universal natural rights (with the assumption of equality) alongside rights that come about with the occupation of a particular role or status (e.g., parent, master, sovereign).

The Alienability of Natural Rights

Another important aspect of Grotius's theory is his stance on the alienability of natural rights. This has significant implications for particular natural rights such as the right to defend and preserve ourselves. Grotius argues that this right must be given up to the sovereign.

> All men have naturally a Right to secure themselves from Injuries by Resistance. . . . But civil Society being instituted for the Preservation of Peace, there immediately arises a superior Right in the state over us and ours, so far as is necessary for that End. Therefore the State has a Power to prohibit the unlimited Use of the Right towards every other Person, for maintaining Publick Peace and good Order, which doubtless it does, since otherwise it cannot obtain the End proposed; for if that Promiscuous Right of Resistance should be allowed, there would be *no longer a State*, but a Multitude without Union.[42]

He acknowledges the distinction between rights that apply to all and those that apply only to those in a particular role, in this case the sovereign or state, in the following way.

> Right, strictly taken, is again twofold, the one, PRIVATE, established for the advantage of each individual, the other SUPERIOR, as involving the claims, which the state has upon individuals, and their property, for the public good. Thus . . . the Sovereign has a greater right over the property of his subjects, where the public good is concerned, than the owners themselves have.[43]

What is important here, rather than the distinction between rights held by all and rights held only by a person or persons in a role, is the question of the alienability of rights. Grotius makes clear that all natural rights, including those to self-defence and resistance as well as property, are alienable and that they cannot be held against the sovereign.

Concluding Thoughts on Grotius

We can see from the quotations above that Grotius meshes together several different strands of thinking on rights. On the one hand he reasserts the old objective use of the term "right" as simply meaning "what is just according to natural law" and on the other he asserts the new subjective understanding of "rights" as attached to individuals, marking out an area of justified claims and freedoms that are due to each subject or citizen. He also includes in his analysis of subjective rights, those that only apply to individuals occupying a particular status or role.

It is clear, then, that there are elements to his thinking that mark him out as less than a *fully-fledged natural rights theorist*, at least in the Lockean sense, which might be characterized as the view that natural rights are universal moral rights that attach to all individuals, some of which are inalienable and that governments have duties to protect such rights. Grotius's position on the alienability of rights, his argument that certain important rights, including those to self-defence and self-preservation, can and must be given up to the sovereign, means that these crucial natural rights last only until the sovereign is in place. In short, according to Grotius, there are no individual rights of self-defence or self-preservation once we are members of a state. It is not surprising then, that Grotius's arguments were taken up by absolutists, as Tuck mentions, and also not surprising that similar arguments were used by the royalists during the English Civil War. We could say that in this way the *language* of natural rights can be used by absolutists to render impotent the radical idea that all people have natural rights (some of which are inalienable), and that those rights should be respected and protected.

Given the conflicting strains within Grotius's theory we can see the source for Tuck's argument that Grotius stands at the beginning of a fork in the road for natural rights theories, with one branch leading to what he has termed a conservative, authoritarian strain in some theories of natural rights and the other fork to the more typically understood liberal natural rights theories. "Grotius was both the first conservative rights theorist in Protestant Europe and also, in a sense, the first radical rights theorist."[44] I do not agree with Tuck's argument, particularly as he applies it to Hobbes. He argues that Hobbes is one of the "conservative" rights theorists, albeit as "a somewhat deviant member" of the group. This group is characterized by Tuck as "condoning slavery and absolutism." I will not address Tuck's argument in detail here but it will become clear that my interpretation of Hobbes's theory of rights differs significantly from his. I do agree, however, with Tuck's more general point that in Grotius we find a theory of natural rights with significant conservative strains that marks it out from the more radical version that becomes so important in liberal theory.

NATURAL RIGHTS IN POLITICAL DISCOURSE

Arguments about natural rights take place in theoretical debates about political arrangements throughout the late medieval period, in which the notion of subjective rights first emerges, and on into the early modern period. Tierney discusses debates before Ockham that are then taken up by him concerning the alienability of rights and the related question of "the proper limits of ruling authority."[45] He points out that at this time the "idea of natural rights could be used to defend either absolutist or liberal theories of government; the outcome of the argument turned on the theory of alienability that an author adopted. The question at issue was whether the members of a community could or actually did alienate all their rights in the act of constituting a government. If they did so they would have instituted an absolutist government."[46] I would put the same point slightly differently and say that the version of natural rights theory that says all (or some crucial) natural rights can and must be given up to the sovereign is a manipulation of the idea that all people have natural rights. It takes away what is new and significant about the idea of natural rights that replaces old notions of natural hierarchy with the idea that people are equal, with equal moral status and therefore hold equal rights.

By the time of the English Civil War in the 1640s, the language of natural rights is common and familiar and is used by both sides in the conflict but in very different ways. On the part of the royalists, it was used in the way I have just described, to justify absolutism. When it was used by the parliamentarians, and particularly by the Levellers, it was used in the radical sense of early natural rights thinkers like Las Casas. Once fully developed in political theory, most famously by Locke, it captures the notion that natural rights are universal, often inalienable, rights that must be protected by the state. It was this idea of natural rights that took hold and culminated in the justifications of revolutions in America and France and it is the same idea that is recognised in the contemporary notion of "human rights."[47] That is why I have categorised Grotius's theory of natural rights as falling short of a *fully-fledged natural rights theory*. The next section will look at the use of natural rights language in the political writings of those on either side of the English Civil War.

The Use of Natural Rights Arguments in the Political Writing of the English Civil War

During this period, the two sides in the conflict put forward two distinct ways of dealing with the notion that individuals possess natural rights. Roughly speaking, the royalists argue that all natural rights of individuals are given up to the sovereign or that the sovereign distributes natural rights as he sees fit. Natural rights, if they exist, are all alienable, they can all be given up and indeed must be given up because to retain them would be to pose a challenge to the authority and power of the sovereign.

Royalists

As Sir Robert Filmer puts it in *Patriarcha*, "all those liberties that are claimed in parliaments are the liberties of grace from the king, and not the liberties of nature to the people. For if the liberty were retained it would give power to the multitude to assemble themselves *when* and *where* they please, to bestow sovereignty and by pactions to limit and direct the exercise of it."[48] And it is worth noting that the subtitle to *Patriarcha* begins "*The Natural Power of Kings Defended Against the Unnatural Liberty of the People. . . .*" This makes clear the political position of the absolutists against notions that all individuals have natural rights (liberties). It is only the sovereign who really has rights—they are his to distribute as he chooses, to his subjects. The subjects are never justified in retaining any rights or in using them to resist the sovereign.

Filmer argues in *Patriarcha* for divine right theory and explicitly attacks the notion I have been discussing "first hatched in the schools" that "Mankind is naturally endowed and born with freedom from all subjection, and at liberty to choose what form of government it please."[49] As the arguments for natural rights were becoming commonplace, there was political resistance to them on the part of those proclaiming the virtues of political absolutism and a natural hierarchy. Natural rights arguments threatened the political order that the absolutists were seeking to defend.

The more moderate royalists also argued that natural rights should be given up to the sovereign. This is particularly important concerning the right to self-defence and the question of whether it could be held against the king. Dudley Digges, a member of the so-called Tew Circle of intellectuals, argues, in a posthumously published pamphlet, that the right to self-preservation is not a law but merely a right of nature which can be given up as all natural rights can be given up.[50] As we have seen, even Grotius, who is considered one of the great natural rights theorists of the time, argues that the right to self-defence can and must be given up to the sovereign.

Parliamentarians

The moderate parliamentarians, in opposition to the absolutism of Charles 1, argue that the right to self-defence can be retained and held, even against the king. They did not go so far as to say that individuals could retain rights against Parliament, however. So, their position is somewhat equivocal. For example, Charles Herle argues that "The Parliament is the people's own consent, which once passed, they cannot revoke. . . ."[51]

Radical parliamentarian groups such as the Levellers were much clearer in their support for the notion of inalienable natural rights. The following rights are said by the Levellers to be inalienable: the right to change the government if it fails to protect the people, the right to be treated equally under the law, the right to choose one's religion, the right to defend and preserve oneself, the right not to fight in a war. John Lilburne says,

> . . . though Kings or Parliaments may confirme unto the people their rights, freedoms and liberties; yet it lies not in their power to take them from them againe when they please; no not at all: because all betrusted powers are (as both Kings and Parliaments, and all other Magistrates whatsoever are,) & ought always to be, for the good of the Trusters, and not for their mischief and hurt.[52]

This view of rights has a lot in common with what Locke agues forty years later and which comes to be accepted as the classic expression of natural rights theory. It is clear from this brief glance at the use of natural rights arguments in political discourse in the sixteenth and seventeenth centuries that the idea that each individual human being has natural rights, some of which are inalienable, becomes a potent political weapon. And it is in the eighteenth century that it informs and justifies two revolutions and sets the stage for liberal political thought for centuries to come.

THE CULMINATION OF A POLITICAL IDEA— JOHN LOCKE'S THEORY OF NATURAL RIGHTS

Locke starts his argument for government in the *Second Treatise* with a reminder to the reader that he has, in the *First Treatise*, argued against the political absolutism and divine right theory of Sir Robert Filmer. "It having been shown in the foregoing discourse, 1. That *Adam* had not, either by natural right of fatherhood, or by positive donation from God, any such authority over his children, or dominion over the world, as is pretended: 2. That if he had, his heirs, yet, had no right to it:"[53] Locke is going to argue that political authority comes from the people and exists in order to protect their rights. His argument starts by positing a state of nature which he describes as a state where individuals are free in a political sense but not free from the moral law, that is, from the law of nature. The following passage illustrates this and the fact that Locke uses theological premises in his argument for natural rights.

> . . . [T]hough this be a *state of liberty*, yet *it is not a state of license*: . . . though man in that state have an uncontroulable liberty to dispose of his person or possessions, yet he has not liberty to destroy himself, . . . The *state of nature* has a law of nature to govern it, which obliges every one: and reason, which is

that law, teaches all mankind, who will but consult it, that being all *equal and independent,* no one ought to harm another in his life, health, liberty, or possessions: for men being all the workmanship of one omnipotent, and infinitely wise maker; all the servants of one sovereign master, sent into the world by his order, and about his business; they are his property, whose workmanship they are, made to last during his, not one another's pleasure: and being furnished with like faculties, sharing all in one community of nature, there cannot be supposed any such *subordination* among us, that may authorize us to destroy one another, as if we were made for one another's uses, as the inferior ranks of creatures are for our's.

He then moves to a statement of natural rights.

> Every one, as he is *bound to preserve himself,* and not to quit his station wilfully, so by the like reason, when his own preservation comes not in competition, ought he, as much as he can, *to preserve the rest of mankind,* and may not, unless it be to do justice on an offender, take away, or impair the life, or what tends to the preservation of the life, the liberty, health, limb, or goods of another.
>   And that all men may be restrained from invading others rights.[54]

So, in a natural state, before the institution of a government, "all men" are naturally in "a state of perfect freedom to order their actions and dispose of their possessions and persons as they think fit, within the bounds of the law of nature, without asking leave or depending upon the will of any other man."[55] And the state of nature is also "[a] state of *equality.*"[56] And in Chapter iv he tells us that we cannot enslave ourselves.

> This freedom from absolute, arbitrary power, is so necessary to, and joined with a man's preservation, that he cannot part with it, . . . for a man, not having the power of his own life, *cannot,* by compact, or his own consent, enslave himself to any one, nor put himself under the absolute arbitrary power of another to take away his life, when he pleases.[57]

Locke is arguing, in other words, that our natural rights to life and to the most basic liberty are inalienable. The reason he gives for this is that only God has the power over life and death. He then argues that we can only leave the state of nature and put ourselves under a government if we consent to do so.

MEN being, as has been said, by nature, all free, equal, and independent, no one can be put out of this estate, and subjected to the political power of another, without his own consent. The only way whereby any one divests himself of his natural liberty, and puts on the *bonds of civil society,* is by

agreeing with other men to join and unite into a community for their comfortable, safe, and peaceable living one amongst another, . . .[58]

Once a government is instituted by the people with their agreement and
consent it has the right to govern and legislate. "When any number of men
have so *consented to make one community or government,* they are thereby
presently incorporated and make *one body politic,* wherein the *majority*
have a right to act and conclude the rest."[59] If the government acts "contrary to their trust" then it is dissolved. For example, if the *"legislative
acts against the trust* reposed in them, when they endeavour to invade the
property of the subject, and to make themselves, or any part of the community, masters or arbitrary disposers of the lives, liberties, or fortunes of
the people."[60]

Once the people's rights are violated by the government then the people
have the right to rebel and dissolve the government. He goes on, "by this
breach of trust they *forfeit the power* the people had put into their hands for
quite contrary ends, and it devolves to the people; who have a right to resume
their original liberty, and, by the establishment of a new legislative (such as
they think fit), provide for their own safety and security, which is the end for
which they are in society."[61] Here we have the classical version of natural
rights theory that was to come to dominate liberal political theory and to be
seen as the forerunner of modern theories of individual rights and human
rights. The theory's clear dependence on theological premises and natural
law theory will be discussed in chapter 3. The current discussion concerns
the core ideas of natural rights as applied to political theory by Locke. These
core ideas include: the notion that all individuals have (subjective) rights that
attach to them originally, the assumption that all individuals are equal and the
notion that certain important rights are inalienable. When these natural rights
principles are then applied by Locke to a theory of government, the result is
an argument that in a state of nature all are free and equal and endowed with
natural rights and that governments are formed by mutual consent (literal or
tacit) to protect those rights. Some rights/liberties are given up as the restrictions of living in society under law are accepted but important rights to life,
property, basic liberty, self-defence, and self-preservation are retained, being
inalienable.

Governments are entrusted with the power to govern by individuals seeking to protect their rights and if governments fail to protect the people's
rights, then they can be dissolved and the people return to a state of natural
liberty, free to form a new government. These core ideas are those that inspire
and justify the revolutions in America and France in the following century
and provide the blueprint for their and many other new constitutions. They
also come to be dominant in political discourse as modern "liberal" ideas
gradually replace those of monarchy and absolutism.

American Declaration of Independence—July 4, 1776

In 1776 the leaders of the American Revolution in declaring independence from the British Crown, made their Lockean principles central to their argument for independence.

> When in the Course of human events, it becomes necessary for one people to dissolve the political bands which have connected them with another, and to assume among the powers of the earth, the separate and equal station to which the Laws of Nature and of Nature's God entitle them, a decent respect to the opinions of mankind requires that they should declare the causes which impel them to the separation.
>
> We hold these truths to be self-evident, that all men are created equal, that they are endowed by their Creator with certain unalienable Rights, that among these are Life, Liberty and the pursuit of Happiness.—That to secure these rights, Governments are instituted among Men, deriving their just powers from the consent of the governed,—That whenever any Form of Government becomes destructive of these ends, it is the Right of the People to alter or to abolish it, and to institute new Government, laying its foundation on such principles and organizing its powers in such form, as to them shall seem most likely to affect their Safety and Happiness.[62]

French Declaration of the Rights of Man

Approved by the National Assembly of France, August 26, 1789

The representatives of the French people, organized as a National Assembly, believing that the ignorance, neglect, or contempt of the rights of man are the sole cause of public calamities and of the corruption of governments, have determined to set forth in a solemn declaration the natural, unalienable, and sacred rights of man, in order that this declaration, being constantly before all the members of the Social body, shall remind them continually of their rights and duties; in order that the acts of the legislative power, as well as those of the executive power, may be compared at any moment with the objects and purposes of all political institutions and may thus be more respected, and, lastly, in order that the grievances of the citizens, based hereafter upon simple and incontestable principles, shall tend to the maintenance of the constitution and redound to the happiness of all. Therefore the National Assembly recognizes and proclaims, in the presence and under the auspices of the Supreme Being, the following rights of man and of the citizen:

Articles:

1. Men are born and remain free and equal in rights. Social distinctions may be founded only upon the general good.
2. The aim of all political association is the preservation of the natural and imprescriptible rights of man. These rights are liberty, property, security, and resistance to oppression.
4. Liberty consists in the freedom to do everything which injures no one else; hence the exercise of the natural rights of each man has no limits except those which assure to the other members of the society the enjoyment of the same rights. These limits can only be determined by law.
17. Since property is an inviolable and sacred right, no one shall be deprived thereof except where public necessity, legally determined, shall clearly demand it, and then only on condition that the owner shall have been previously and equitably indemnified.[63]

These quotations from the American Declaration of Independence and the French Declaration of the Rights of Man, illustrate the way in which the radical new ideas, captured in the development of notions of natural rights in the early work of writers such as Las Casas and refined within the political theory of John Locke, have come to be widely known and powerful moral and political ideas by the late eighteenth century. Despite the diminishing power and influence of the theological elements of natural rights theory, the core ideas of equality and inviolable rights attached to all humans, continue to dominate liberal political discourse and theory at least to the end of the twentieth century. This is despite the rupture in the philosophical justification of natural rights which will be the subject of the next chapter.

NOTES

1. Richard Tuck, *Natural Rights Theories: Their Origin and Development* (Cambridge: Cambridge University Press, 1979), A. P. d'Entreves, *Natural Law, An Introduction to Legal Philosophy* (London: Hutchinson and Co., 1951).

2. Brian Tierney, "The Idea of Natural Rights-Origins and Persistence," *North Western Journal of Human Rights* 1 (2004), 3/4.

3. Brian Tierney, *The Idea of Natural Rights* (Atlanta, GA: Scholars Press for Emory University, 1997), Ch. 1.

4. Silvestro Mazzolini da Prierio, *Summa Summarum quae Silvestrina nuncupatur* (Bologna, 1515), quoted in Tuck, *Natural Rights Theories*, 5.

5. Rowan Cruft, S. Mathew Liao and Massimo Renzo, *Philosophical Foundations of Human Rights* (Oxford: Oxford University Press, 2015), 1.

6. John Locke, *Second Treatise of Government* (1690), ed. C. B. Macpherson (Indianapolis: Hackett Publishing Company Inc., 1980), 9.

7. Locke, *Second Treatise of Government*, 9.

8. Tierney, "The Idea of Natural Rights-Origins and Persistence," 4.

9. Leo Strauss, *The Political Philosophy of Hobbes. Its Basis and Its Genesis* (1936) transl. Elsa M Sinclair (Chicago: University of Chicago Press, 1952, Midway Reprint 1984), viii.

10. "RIGHT, consisteth in liberty to do, or to forbeare"; Thomas Hobbes, *Leviathan* (1651), ed. C B Macpherson (London: Penguin Books, 1968), 189.

11. Hobbes, *Leviathan*, 189.

12. Thomas Hobbes, *On the Citizen* (1647), ed. Richard Tuck and Michael Silverthorne (Cambridge: Cambridge University Press, 1998) 156.

13. Tierney, *The Idea of Natural Rights*, 32.

14. Tierney, *The Idea of Natural Rights*, 33.

15. Tierney, "The Idea of Natural Rights-Origins and Persistence," 8.

16. Tierney, "The Idea of Natural Rights-Origins and Persistence," 5.

17. Tierney, *The Idea of Natural Rights*, 16.

18. Tierney, "The Idea of Natural Rights-Origins and Persistence," 7.

19. Cicero, *De Re Publica*, III, xxii, cited in d'Entreves, *Natural Law*, 20, 21.

20. See Brian Tierney, *The Idea of Natural Rights*, for an illuminating discussion of Las Casas's arguments on natural rights and his use of both Thomistic and Aristotelian texts as well as ancient legal texts to support his arguments.

21. "Even if a majority freely consented to accept an alien king's rule, since they acted against liberty their action could not prejudice a dissenting minority; in such a case the opinion of a minority refusing consent should prevail. All this amounted to a very extreme defence of the individual right to liberty." Tierney, *The Idea of Natural Rights*, 285.

22. Las Casas, quoted in Tierney, *The Idea of Natural Rights*, 278.

23. Las Casas, quoted in Tierney, *The Idea of Natural Rights*, 278.

24. Tierney, *The idea of Natural Rights*, 284.

25. Las Casas, quoted in Tierney, *The Idea of Natural Rights*, 284.

26. Tierney, *The Idea of Natural Rights*, 285.

27. Tierney, *The Idea of Natural Rights*, 285.

28. Tierney, *The Idea of Natural Rights*, 286/287.

29. "Now the Law of Nature is so unalterable, that it cannot be changed even by God himself. For although the power of God is infinite, yet there are some things, to which it does not extend. Because the things so expressed would have no true meaning, but imply a contradiction. Thus two and two must make four, nor is it possible to be otherwise; nor, again, can what is really evil not be evil." Hugo Grotius, *The Rights of War and Peace (De Iure Belli ac Pacis,* Paris, 1625), Adamant Media Corp., 2005 (unabridged facsimile of M. Walter Dunne edn. Washington and London, 1901), 22.

30. John Finnis, *Natural Law and Natural Rights* (Oxford: Oxford University Press, 1980).

31. Grotius says that we are given "sovereign reason" by God, who "imprinted on man the image of his own mind," Grotius, *De jure Praedae*, 8, quoted in Tierney, *The Idea of Natural Rights*, 327.

32. Grotius, *The Rights of War and Peace*, 22.

33. Tierney, *The Idea of Natural Rights*, 320.

34. Grotius, *The Rights of War and Peace*, 18.

35. Grotius, *The Rights of War and Peace*, 21.

36. Grotius, *The Rights of War and Peace*, 19.

37. Grotius, *The Rights of War and Peace*, 19.

38. Grotius, *The Rights of War and Peace*, 19.

39. Grotius, *De Iure Belli ac Pacis* (Paris 1625), vol. Prolegomena, 8–10, quoted in Tuck, *Natural Rights Theories*, 72/73.

40. Grotius, *De Iure Belli ac Pacis*, I, II, I, 5 (Paris 1625), quoted in Tuck, *Natural Rights Theories*, 73.

41. Grotius, *The Rights of War and Peace*, 19.

42. Grotius, *De Iure Belli ac Pacis*, I, IV, II, I (Paris 1625) quoted in Tuck, *Natural Rights Theories*, 78/79.

43. Grotius, *The Rights of War and Peace*, 20.

44. Tuck, *Natural Rights Theories*, 71.

45. Tierney, *The Idea of Natural Rights*, 182.

46. Tierney, *The Idea of Natural Rights*, 182/183.

47. "Whereas recognition of the inherent dignity and of the equal and inalienable rights of all members of the human family is the foundation of freedom, justice and peace in the world," Preamble, *Universal Declaration of Human Rights*, United Nations General Assembly, Paris, December 1948.

48. J. P. Sommerville, ed., *Sir Robert Filmer, Patriarcha and Other Writings* (Cambridge: Cambridge University Press. 1991), 55.

49. Sommerville, *Sir Robert Filmer, Patriarcha and Other Writings*, 2.

50. See discussion of Dudley Digges, *The Unlawfulness of Subjects Taking up Arms Against the Sovereign* (London: 1644), in Tuck, *Natural Rights Theories*, 102/103.

51. F. D. Dow, *Radicalism in the English Revolution 1640–1660* (Oxford: Basil Blackwell, 1985), 18.

52. John Lilburne, *The Charters of London, or, the Second Part of Londons Liberty in Chains Discovered* (London: 1646) title page. University of Oxford, 2011.

53. Locke, *Second Treatise of Government*, 7.

54. Locke, *Second Treatise of Government*, 9.

55. Locke, *Second Treatise of Government*, 8.

56. Locke, *Second Treatise of Government*, 8.

57. Locke, *Second Treatise of Government*, 17.

58. Locke, *Second Treatise of Government*, 52.

59. Locke, *Second Treatise of Government*, 52.

60. Locke, *Second Treatise of Government*, 111.

61. Locke, *Second Treatise of Government*, 111.

62. *The American Declaration of Independence*, 1776. https://www.archives.gov/founding-docs/declaration-transcript.

63. *French Declaration of the Rights of Man*, 1789. https://constitutionnet.org/sites/default/files/declaration_of_the_rights_of_man_1789.pdf.

Chapter 2

The Philosophical Discrediting of Natural Law and Natural Rights

HUME'S ATTACK ON NATURAL LAW

Before the leaders of either the American or French Revolutions had made natural rights their justifying principle, David Hume had published what would come to be seen as a devastating attack on natural law theory. This marked the beginning of the philosophical unravelling of natural law theory and consequently of the undermining of theories of natural rights which were seen as coming out of and being philosophically dependent upon, theories of natural law.

Hume's attack on natural law theory is framed as an argument against the logical validity of the theory. The way that natural law theory argues to its conclusions breaks a basic rule of logic, according to Hume and therefore those conclusions cannot be accepted. In this famous passage he sets out his claim.

> In every system of morality, which I have hitherto met with, . . . the author proceeds for some time in the ordinary way of reasoning, and establishes the being of a God, or makes observations concerning human affairs; when of a sudden I am surpriz'd to find, that instead of the usual copulations of propositions , *is,* and *is not,* I meet with no proposition that is not connected with an *ought,* or *ought not.* This change is imperceptible; but is, however, of the last consequence. For as this *ought,* or *ought not*, expresses some new relation or affirmation, 'tis necessary that it should be observed and explain'd; and at the same time that a reason should be given, for what seems altogether inconceivable, how this new relation can be a deduction from the others, which are entirely different from it.[1]

Hume's simple point about the logic involved in making deductive arguments proved to be a powerful criticism of natural law theory, demonstrating its apparent vulnerability to what came to be known as the "is/ought problem."[2] This criticism, in its simplest and most straightforward version as describing an error of logic, was largely accepted, and regarded as damaging to the philosophical standing of natural law theory. As J. W. Harris puts it, "for many jurists, Hume's point is a knock down argument against all forms of natural law thinking";[3] Provided that one accepts Hume's analysis that natural law theory takes factual premises about the nature of human beings and then deduces moral conclusions from those factual statements, it is hard to deny the force of his argument.

The more general argument underlying Hume's criticism is one that seeks to demonstrate that morality comes not from reason but from the emotions, the argument being that only emotions can motivate us to action. This is closely tied to his project of submitting all claims to knowledge to empirical scrutiny and scepticism. John Finnis comments on Hume's famous passage above in the following way,

> There have been many interpretations of this passage, but it will be safe to attend here only to the two most plausible. The first and standard interpretation treats Hume as announcing the logical truth, widely emphasized since the later part of the nineteenth century, that no set of non-moral (or, more generally, non-evaluative) premises can entail a moral (or evaluative) conclusion. The second interpretation places the passage in its historical and literary context, and sees it as the tailpiece to Hume's attack on the eighteenth century rationalists (notably Samuel Clarke), an attack whose centre-piece is the contention that rational perception of the moral qualities of actions could not itself provide a motivating guide to action.[4]

Finnis goes on to say that while the second interpretation "has more to commend it as an interpretation" the "important thing" about the first is that the "logical principle in question" "is true and significant."[5]

The acceptance of the is/ought problem as a serious attack on natural law theory was strengthened by the addition, at the start of the twentieth century, of G. E. Moore's version of the criticism, in the form of the "naturalistic fallacy."[6] Although Moore was primarily addressing his arguments to more contemporary moral theorists, his claim that moral goodness cannot be reduced to or deduced from natural properties, has been taken to be an argument against the validity of natural law and natural rights.[7]

A simple example from natural law theory will serve to illustrate exactly what is being attacked by Hume and his followers. In the following quotation from Locke (extracted from the longer quotation in chapter 1), we can see how natural law moves seamlessly from apparently factual premises, in this case about the equality of all human beings, to moral conclusions, that we should therefore not harm one another or invade one another's rights.

> The *state of nature* has a law of nature to govern it, which obliges every one: and reason, which is that law, teaches all mankind, who will but consult it, that being all *equal* and *independent,* no one ought to harm another in his life, health, liberty, or possessions.[8]

If we take Hume's attack at face value, it seems that natural law's mistake is simply to draw moral conclusions from factual premises. So, for example, according to natural law, we naturally seek to preserve ourselves, therefore, it tells us, we *ought* to preserve ourselves. It is morally right for us to preserve ourselves, merely because we are inclined by nature to do so. And this does seem to be a simple example of a logical mistake, deriving conclusions from premises that do not contain those conclusions; that is, drawing moral conclusions from factual premises. Something the criticism leaves unsaid, is the question of the theology lying behind natural law theory. The reason such natural inclinations as self-preservation are said to be morally justified is because they come from God; an unimpeachable moral authority. A quotation from Aquinas illustrates this point. ". . . it is clear that the whole community of the universe is governed by the divine reason. This rational guidance of created things on the part of God . . . we can call the Eternal law."

> [Now] since all things which are subject to divine Providence are measured and regulated by the Eternal law . . . it is clear that all things participate to some degree in the Eternal law, in so far as they derive from it certain inclinations to those actions and aims which are proper to them.
>
> But, of all others, rational creatures are subject to divine Providence in a very special way; being themselves made participators in Providence itself, in that they control their own actions and the actions of others. So they have a certain share in the divine reason itself, deriving therefrom a natural inclination to such actions and ends as are fitting. This participation in the Eternal law by rational creatures is called the Natural Law.[9]

Hume's attack on natural law theory can be seen as part of a more general attack by the empiricists upon any philosophical system or argument that relies on theological or metaphysical premises. This aspect of the attack, however, is not stated explicitly as part of the "logical" criticism that forms such an important part of the history I am recounting. In most accounts of the discrediting of natural law theory, no mention is made of this much wider attack on metaphysical or theological systems and nothing is made, for example, of Hume's own religious scepticism. Recent commentary on Hume does, however, emphasize his scepticism regarding the existence of God.[10]

This adds some historical context to the philosophical arguments as they appear in accounts of the discrediting of natural law theory. The philosophical criticism of natural law theory coincides with a period in which the hitherto universally accepted assumptions of Christian theology within Western philosophy are starting to loosen. It becomes possible to question theological premises which had been incontrovertible during the medieval period and into the early modern period. It gradually becomes more common to attack philosophical theories that rely on premises that are seen to fail empirical (and/or logical) tests.

THE DISCREDITING OF NATURAL LAW
SPREADS TO NATURAL RIGHTS

These attacks on *natural law* were also significant for the standing of theories of *natural rights*. Once the philosophical basis of *natural law theory* was under attack it did not take long before the scepticism spread to *theories of natural rights*, which had developed within the philosophical orbit of natural law. It is in the writings of Jeremy Bentham that natural rights find their sharpest and most influential critic. Indeed, Bentham's infamous remark that the notion of natural and imprescriptible rights is "nonsense upon stilts" is still widely quoted today.[11]

Bentham applies Hume's attack on natural law theory to philosophy of law as well as to moral theory. On language, Bentham takes the view that general or abstract words and phrases do not represent reality but describe fictitious entities. When this nominalist approach is applied to natural law, it can be argued that the theological or metaphysical premises do not refer to anything real and to this is added Hume's criticism that factual premises about human nature cannot entail moral conclusions. Natural law theory, as a theory of *law*, Bentham argues, confuses what the law *is* with what the law *ought to be*. Applying the same rigorous empirical scepticism to law that Hume had to morality, he argues that law is a matter of verifiable, empirical fact and cannot therefore contain theological or metaphysical premises or statements of moral judgement. It cannot be the case that if a manmade law clashes with natural law it is in some sense not really law, as claimed in the declaration of St Augustine that "an unjust law is no law at all."[12] Here we have the beginnings of the legal positivism that Bentham was to develop with John Austin, according to which there is no necessary connection of law to morality, in contrast to natural law theory, which states that there is such a connection. What the Law *is*, argue the positivists, is a matter of fact, while statements about whether the law is *just* are part of a separate exercise in moral judgement. For Bentham, morality itself also has to be grounded in factual reality and is, as he argues in his theory of utilitarianism, with its reliance on human pleasure as both a factual and moral good. (Some attacked utilitarianism for itself being an example of the naturalistic fallacy).

Bentham's attack on the idea of natural rights is closely tied to his criticism of natural law and his insistence that law is a matter of social fact. For him, the idea of natural rights, just like natural law in general, refers to nothing real. Rights, according to Bentham, can only exist when created by law, "right is with me the child of law: . . . A natural right is a son that never had a father."[13]

It is hardly surprising, given Bentham's insistence that rights can only exist in law, combined with the philosophical discrediting of theories of natural law by Hume, Bentham, Moore, and their empiricist and positivist followers,[14] that the philosophy of rights takes a jurisprudential turn. Bentham's insistence that rights can only exist in law, combined with the influence of the new positivism leads to attempts by a new generation of analytical jurists to explain and justify individual rights. Once the philosophical theories that natural rights are (seen as) dependent upon, are out of favour and perceived as discredited, some other philosophical explanation of individual rights is required, if the idea is to survive and to have a philosophical justification. One interesting aspect of this history is that the idea of individual rights does survive all the philosophical criticism and uncertainty and indeed the idea has only gained in strength and acceptance at least in political and legal discourse. As Margaret MacDonald puts it,

> Doctrines on natural law and natural rights have a long and impressive history from the Stoics and Roman jurists to the Atlantic Charter and Roosevelt's Four Freedoms. That men are entitled to make certain claims by virtue simply of their common humanity has been equally and passionately defended and vehemently denied. Punctured by the cool scepticism of Hume; routed by the contempt of Bentham for "nonsense upon stilts"; submerged by idealist and Marxist philosophers in the destiny of the totalitarian state; the claim to "natural rights" has never quite been defeated.[15]

I would rephrase this last statement to say that the claim to "individual rights" has never been defeated. It has been reclaimed and repackaged particularly by jurists seeking to find new explanations and justifications for the notion that individuals have rights, after the jettisoning of the theological and metaphysical "baggage" of natural law and natural rights theory. One of the most surprising aspects of the persistence of the idea of individual rights is that something very close to the idea of *natural rights* lives on in the modern notion of *human rights*. Philosophical justifications for *human rights* will be examined in Chapter Seven. The jurisprudential turn in the philosophy of rights will be examined in chapter 4.

Marx's Criticism of Individual Rights

It is worth briefly mentioning the opposition to the idea of individual rights that comes from Marxist commentaries. While these criticisms do not form a major part of the philosophical history of rights theory, they have been influential on the political discourse and theorizing of those influenced by Marxist theory. Many commentators on the left remain, to some degree, sceptical of the idea of individual rights claims.[16]

Marx addresses the question of individual rights in his essay "On the Jewish Question," written when he was a young man in 1843. He is responding to the argument of Bruno Bauer against Jewish emancipation. Bauer's argument is that political emancipation for Jews is not justified on the ground that it is incompatible with religious practice. Marx argues that political emancipation is perfectly compatible with religion and that this has been demonstrated in the US where Jews have political rights, while still being free to practice their religion. But Marx goes on to argue that *political* emancipation (the grant of liberal rights and liberties), is both insufficient to bring about the ultimate goal of *human emancipation* and in some sense, a barrier to it. In the course of his argument Marx makes the following statement on individual rights.

> But liberty as a right of man is not founded upon the relations between man and man, but rather upon the separation of man from man. It is the right of such separation. The right of the circumscribed individual, withdrawn into himself.[17]

This remark captures the fundamental objection to ideas of individual rights made by Marx and many of his followers, in terms of its perceived promotion of a fundamentally individualistic analysis of society that is incompatible with Marxist philosophy.

THE DEFENCE OF NATURAL LAW AND NATURAL RIGHTS

Despite the general acceptance of the philosophical arguments, outlined above, against theories of natural law and natural rights; the theories are not without their defenders. The most important modern defence of natural law and natural rights comes, arguably, from John Finnis, who attacks Hume's criticism and offers his own modern version of natural law and natural rights theory. Despite the apparently ubiquitous rejection of natural law theory within Anglo-American academic philosophy (with the exception of Catholic philosophy and teaching), Finnis's 1980 book, *Natural law and Natural Rights*, provides a defence that is certainly respected, if not widely accepted. I shall outline Finnis's argument here to demonstrate that a modern philosophical defence of natural law theory is possible even though it remains extremely unlikely that any such defence will turn the tide back towards an acceptance of natural law thinking.

Finnis declares his intention to put forward a theory of natural law without theological premises. "Part II of this book offers a rather elaborate sketch of a theory of natural law without needing to advert to the question of God's existence or nature or will."[18] He picks out seven basic, "forms of good" which are, he argues, presupposed by human action and human life. The crux of his defence against Hume's argument is that natural law sets out what is self-evidently good for persons *given our nature*, not *deduced from* facts about our nature. In response to the many writers who say, following Hume, that natural law theory claims that fundamental principles regarding good and evil can be inferred from facts about the nature of man, Finnis argues that the first principles of natural law can be grasped by anyone of the age of reason and are self-evident and indemonstrable.[19] What is more, he says, contrary to the attacks of the critics,

> the first principles of natural law . . . are not inferred from speculative principles. They are not inferred from facts. They are not inferred from metaphysical propositions about human nature, or about the nature of good and evil, or about "the function of a human being," nor are they inferred from a teleological conception of nature or any other concept of nature. They are not inferred or derived from anything.
>
> And finally, he concludes, ". . . the objection that Aquinas's account of natural law proposes an illicit inference from "is" to "ought" is quite unjustified."[20]

Finnis argues that we understand what is good for humans, not from the outside by observation, but from the inside, "in the form of one's inclinations" without any process of inference.

> One does not judge that "I have [or everybody has] an inclination to find out about things" and then infer that therefore "knowledge is a good to be pursued." Rather, by a simple act of non-inferential understanding one grasps that the object of the inclination which one experiences is an instance of a general form of good, for oneself (and others like one).[21]

A little more detail may help to flesh out Finnis's argument. The seven forms of good Finnis picks out are life, knowledge, play, aesthetic experience, sociability (friendship), practical reasonableness, and religion. Each of the seven, according to Finnis, defines a basic (irreducible) form of human activity or human value that we all recognize as goods. Practical reasonableness is itself one of the seven forms of good and requirements of practical reasonableness guide us in what we choose to do and move us into the realm of morality and natural law. Reasonableness, Finnis argues, "both *is* a basic aspect of human well-being and *concerns* one's participation in all the (other) basic aspects of human well-being. Hence its requirements concern fullness of well-being." This fullness of well-being fulfils Aristotelian notions of goodness (someone who lives up to such requirements has eudaimonia) and fits with Aquinas's version of natural law theory as "we could say that the requirements to which we now turn express the 'natural law method' of working out the (moral) 'natural law' from the first (pre-moral) 'principles of natural law.'"[22]

It is not possible in this discussion to address the finer points of Finnis's argument, which is complex and detailed, but on the broad thrust of the repost to Hume's hugely influential criticism of natural law theory, it is possible to make a couple of points. First, the argument relies on analysing natural law theory in such a way that the case can be made that it does not derive moral conclusions from factual premises. The seven forms of the good are said to be self-evidently good *given our nature* rather than *derived from facts about our nature*. I noted above that Finnis accepts the logical principle that Hume refers to; that in a deductive argument, one cannot deduce conclusions that are of a different type to the statements or propositions contained in the premises of the argument. In his defence of natural law theory Finnis argues, as above, that natural law theory and specifically Aquinas's version of natural law theory does not fall foul of the laws of logic but rather describes forms of good, including practical reasonableness, which enable and indeed require us, to develop an understanding of whether actions are right or wrong. These forms of good describe human values and activities that are self-evidently good for human beings in the sense of being beneficial for human beings. Pursuing such goods, argues Finnis, leads us into the realm of morality. Clearly, this means defining the good as the basic moral value rather than the right. As Rawls puts it,

> The two main concepts of ethics are those of the right and the good. . . . The structure of an ethical theory is, then, largely determined by how it defines and connects these two basic notions. . . . The simplest way of relating them is taken by teleological theories: the good is defined independently from the right and the right is defined as that which maximises the good.[23]

Leaving aside further questions about the relationship of "moral goodness" to other types of goodness (e.g., instrumental goodness) and provided one accepts that the arguments of Finnis, and others like him, do succeed in demonstrating that natural law builds its moral requirements out of human goods that are irrefutable and irreducible, then we must allow that they have a case to make against Hume's attack. Does this make any difference to the history of natural rights theory? Not really. The criticisms of Hume, Bentham et al., were generally accepted and theories of natural law and natural rights were seen as discredited. A number of philosophers continued (and continue) their work in natural law theory[24] but this work is unlikely to bring about a reversal of the perceived loss of credibility within mainstream analytical philosophy regarding theories of natural law. The connection to theological premises persists despite Grotius's, Finnis's and others' efforts to build theories of natural law without recourse to such premises. Mark Murphy, for example, characterizes natural law theories in the following way,

> . . . the paradigmatic natural law view holds that (1) the natural law is given by God; (2) it is naturally authoritative over all human beings; and (3) it is naturally knowable by all human beings. Further, it holds that (4) the good is prior to the right, that (5) right action is action that responds nondefectively to the good, that (6) there are a variety of ways in which action can be defective with respect to the good, and that (7) some of these ways can be captured and formulated as general rules.[25]

The current proponents of natural law theory fail to provide arguments to convince a general philosophical audience that might then justify support for the notion of natural rights. The persistent connection of natural law to *theology* means that natural law theory cannot be defended as a mainstream philosophical theory (in Western philosophy) at the present time. The result is that current *human rights* theory presents multiple justifications of *human rights* that avoid a connection to *natural rights* and natural law, despite acknowledgement of the historical connection of the notion of *human rights* to that of *natural rights*. The recent philosophy of *human rights* will be examined in chapter 7.

NATURAL RIGHTS DO NOT COME FROM OR DEPEND UPON THEORIES OF NATURAL LAW

There is an argument made by some significant commentators that the relationship of natural rights to natural law is not the straightforward one of the standard interpretation, that is, the view that natural rights theories developed from and are dependent upon, traditional theories of natural law. If natural rights do not depend on natural law premises or have a different relationship to natural law than the generally accepted one then this might undermine the attacks of Hume, Bentham et al. In his important 1951 book on natural law, A. P. D'Entrèves declares, that "[o]n the eve of the American and French Revolutions the theory of natural law had been turned into a theory of natural rights."[26] Instead of the usual reading of natural rights emerging from and remaining part of and philosophically dependent upon, natural law, d'Entrèves argues that "[t]he modern theory of natural law was not, properly speaking, a theory of law at all. It was a theory of rights. A momentous change has taken place under cover of the same verbal expressions."[27]

d'Entrèves' argument differs from standard treatments. He takes natural law in a broader sense than is traditionally done and draws a distinction between a historical approach to natural law and a conceptual one. "Another and different approach to our subject can be suggested. Enough evidence has been provided of the historical function of natural law. The time has come to assess its general value."[28] He argues that the early Christian version of natural law is tied to the voluntarist notion of authority coming from the will of God and that Grotius challenges this. "Thus Grotius' famous proposition, that natural law would retain its validity even if God did not exist, once again appears as a turning point in the history of thought. It was the answer to the challenge of voluntarist ethics. It meant the assertion that command is not the essence of law."[29] And he goes on to say that Grotius had "secured a new lease of life for the doctrine of natural law."[30] The new version of natural law provided by Grotius and "his successors" would "prove that it was possible to build up a theory of laws independent of theological presuppositions."[31] Tying this new natural law theory to the equally new social contract theories of political philosophers such as Locke and Hobbes, d'Entrèves concludes that this marks the change in natural law to a theory of natural rights.

The modern theory of natural law "was an assertion of the value of the individual. But it was also and foremost a vindication of rights. As such it could become a theory of revolution."[32] d'Entrèves argues that the natural law link of law to ethics is maintained and so what we have is not something derived from natural law premises but rather a new way of thinking about natural law that emphasizes the individual and their rights. d'Entrèves is advocating the broadest possible view of natural law theory as any theory of law that links law to ethics or morality. This anticipates the work of more recent writers like Dworkin and a jurisprudential approach now more commonly referred to as "non-positivist" rather than "natural law." The central notion is the anti-positivist one that law is, and must be, inextricably linked to morality. d'Entrèves dismisses Hume at the start of the book as pursuing "will-o-the-wisp" investigations of the "divisions and sub-divisions required to cover and account for the infinite varieties of natural law" as these merely provide "arguments for the sceptical denial of natural law as one of the great deceptions of ethics."[33] d'Entrèves is concerned rather to "combine history and philosophy in the study of . . . the vitality of natural law."[34] And this study leads him to see natural rights as the outcome of a vitally important change in thinking.

> . . . it was the vindication of the rights of man which gave modern natural law its tremendous power and vigour. Rationalism, individualism and radicalism combined to give the old word an entirely new meaning. The notion which had been invoked to construct a universal system of law and to provide a rational foundation for ethics, inspired the formulation of a theory of rights which will not easily be cancelled from the heart of Western man and which bears witness to his generosity and idealism.[35]

d'Entrèves is arguing that rather than rejecting traditional natural law theory, as it were, on technical grounds, we should look to the moral values it promotes and particularly to those promoted by natural rights. If we do this, we will recognize the importance and continuing relevance of natural law in the modern form of natural rights.

Leo Strauss also supports the move towards natural rights. His account has some similarities to that of d'Entrèves but with a slightly different emphasis. In *Natural Right and History*[36] he declares, in response to the rejection of traditional notions of natural right, that "the need for natural right is as evident today as it has been for centuries and even millennia. To reject natural right is tantamount to saying that all right is positive right, and this means that what is right is determined exclusively by the legislators and the courts of various countries."[37] Strauss traces the notion of natural right to the questioning of authority by philosophers. Originally, he argues, there was only custom and then from that, came law and with law, authority. He examines the theories of Hobbes and Locke and in a famous reversal of the usual understanding, he argues that Hobbes, instead of deriving natural rights from natural law, starts with natural rights and from that develops his theory of natural law. According to Hobbes, he argues, the basis of morals and politics is not the "law of nature" but the "right of nature."

> Modern and classical political philosophy are fundamentally distinguished in that modern political philosophy takes "right" as its starting-point, whereas classical political philosophy has "law." . . . If modern and classical political philosophy stand in this relation to one another, there is no possible doubt that Hobbes, and no other, is the father of modern political philosophy. For it is he who, with a clarity never previously and never subsequently attained, made the "right of nature," i.e. the justified claims (of the individual) the basis of political philosophy, without any inconsistent borrowing from natural or divine law.[38]

Locke, on the other hand, as I have shown above, does rely on such "borrowing." Strauss admits that Locke is the "most famous and most influential of all modern natural right teachers" but says that it is difficult to gage "how modern he is" or "how much he deviates from the natural right tradition."[39] He puts this down to Locke's "prudence" in a reference to the way in which Locke responded to the political situation at the time he was writing. Strauss is of course famous for arguing that all philosophers' work exists in a complex relationship to the society in which they are living and is necessarily constrained by that relationship. They are aware of the dangers of saying things which are not acceptable in the current political climate and so philosophers write "between the lines."

CONCLUDING THOUGHTS ON THE PHILOSOPHICAL DISCREDITING OF NATURAL LAW AND NATURAL RIGHTS

According to the traditional version of the history of rights theory, the criticisms of Hume, Bentham et al., had a devastating effect on the perceived philosophical credibility of natural law and natural rights. To read historical accounts one would think that the philosophical discrediting of theories of natural rights begins and ends with these writers and that the notion of natural rights has long been dismissed from serious philosophical discussion. As Jeremy Waldron wrote in 2000, "no one now uses the phrase [natural rights] except in a disparaging sense."[40] This may be an exaggeration, but it makes the point that the largely accepted understanding of natural rights today is that they are tied to discredited natural law theories (which are themselves usually tied to theological premises that are untenable in modern Western philosophy) and cannot be taken seriously. This is not to say, however, that the ideas explored within natural rights theory pertaining to the rights themselves, rather than their philosophical justification via natural law, are not still in evidence today. The fundamental idea that there are rights attached to each one of us by virtue of our humanity is a powerful idea that is still very much alive and present, often now of course, in the guise of *human rights*.

After the discrediting of theories of natural rights, the next chapter of the history of rights theory sees philosophers of law take over the task of explaining, analysing and justifying individual rights. This jurisprudential turn will be examined in chapter 4. There is a tension at the heart of mainstream historical accounts of rights theory, which starts with accounts of natural rights and then, despite the philosophical discrediting of natural rights I have outlined above, describes an apparently unbroken progression of notions of individual rights, starting usually with Locke and then developing through modern, secular, jurisprudential accounts of rights.

It is largely accepted that, if forced to choose one writer who provides the blueprint for modern rights theory, particularly for the rights of individuals held against the state, that writer would be John Locke. It is Locke's political theory, with its focus on the rights and consent of the people as central tenets of his social contract theory that provides justifications for the revolutions in America and France and informs the future development of notions of fundamental political rights into the modern age and to the present time. This is usually presented as a seamless progression from Locke's own time to the present day in terms of the development of rights theories. I will take issue with this view of the history of rights theories and argue in the next chapter that if we are looking for a forerunner of modern theories of rights, we should rather look to Hobbes, who provides a much more convincing model than Locke. Hobbes's theory makes no appeal to theological premises or traditional natural law. Just as Locke's theory of natural rights has arguably been over-played as the blueprint for all future theories of individual rights, so Hobbes's theory of rights has, I argue, been underplayed as a valuable contribution to rights theory. The history of rights theory is inclined to ignore the fact that Locke's theory of rights makes direct appeal to natural law and to God as the author of that law and it is equally inclined to ignore the fact that Hobbes's theory of rights makes no such appeal and indeed is free of any theological or metaphysical premises.

NOTES

1. David Hume, *A Treatise of Human Nature*, [1739], ed. Ernest C Mossner (London: Penguin Books, 1969), 521.

2. The criticism refers to the standard deductive syllogism, according to which a conclusion can be deduced from premises so long as nothing new is added. For the argument to be valid the conclusion must already be contained in the premises and the rules of reasoning (getting us from the premises to the conclusion) must be correct. If that is all as it should be then the argument is valid. If, in addition, the premises are true then the conclusion must also be true. A standard example is Aristotle's syllogism—all men are mortal (first premise), Socrates is a man (second premise), therefore Socrates is mortal (conclusion). Hume is claiming that to move from premises containing only statements or propositions of the form "is" and "is not" to conclusions containing statements of the form "ought" or "ought not" is not valid because statements of the form "ought and ought not" are different in kind from statements of the form "is and is not."

3. J. W. Harris, *Legal Philosophies*, second edition (London: Butterworths, 1997), 7.

4. John Finnis, *Natural Law and Natural Rights* (Oxford: Oxford University Press, 1980), 37.

5. Finnis, *Natural Law and Natural Rights*, 37.

6. G. E. Moore, *Principia Ethica* (London: Cambridge University Press, 1903).

7. "To use the language of G. E. Moore, it is always an 'open question' what morally ought to be done given any statement of what is naturally done or factually the case. To think otherwise is to commit what Moore called 'the naturalistic fallacy'—the fallacy of believing that one can derive a theory of what *ought* to be the case from an account of what *is* the case." Jeffrie G Murphy and Jules L Coleman, *Philosophy of Law, An Introduction to Jurisprudence* (London: Westview Press, 1990), 14. "The idea of *natural* rights is seen as a particularly glaring example of the 'Naturalistic Fallacy,' purporting to derive certain norms or evaluations from descriptive premises about human nature." Jeremy Waldron, ed., *Theories of Rights* (Oxford: Oxford University Press, 1984), 3. ". . . many of the attempts to base positive law on an immutably established natural law governing the universe have involved an attempt to link normative rules directly with what are really conjectural hypotheses of factual character. . . . However, in 1740 Hume pointed out the fallacy of trying, as he put it, to derive 'ought' from 'is,' and argued that a normative statement could not be inferred from a purely factual one. So, too, the efforts to define moral norms in terms of something else, which can be ascertained or verified as a fact, . . . involve a similar confusion which has been stigmatised by G. E. Moore as 'the naturalistic fallacy.'" M. D. A. Freeman, *Lloyd's Introduction to Jurisprudence*, Eighth edition (London: Sweet and Maxwell, 2008), 12.

8. Locke, *Second Treatise*, 9.

9. Aquinas, *Summa Theologica*, cited in A. P. d'Entrèves, *Natural Law: An Introduction to Legal Philosophy* (London: Hutchinson and Co. (Publishers) Ltd., 1951), 39.

10. See for example, Russell, Paul and Kraal, Anders, "Hume on Religion," in *The Stanford Encyclopedia of Philosophy* (Summer 2017 Edition) Edward N. Zalta (ed.), https://plato.stanford.edu/archives/sum2017/entries/hume-religion/.

11. "Natural rights is simple nonsense: natural and imprescriptible rights, rhetorical nonsense —nonsense upon stilts." Jeremy Bentham, "Anarchical Fallacies," in *The Works of Jeremy Bentham*, John Bowring ed., Vol. 2 (Edinburgh, 1843).

12. "lex iniusta est non lex," Augustine of Hippo, *De Civitate Dei (City of God)* (Edinburgh: T. & T. Clark, 1871).

13. Jeremy Bentham, *Supply without Burthern* (London: J. Debrett, 1795).

14. For example, Austin, Kelsen, Weber, Hart, Raz.

15. Margaret MacDonald, "Natural Rights," in *Theories of Rights*, ed. Jeremy Waldron (Oxford: Oxford University Press, 1984), 21.

16. See, for example, MacIntyre, Waldron.

17. Karl Marx, On the Jewish Question [1843], 42.

18. John Finnis, *Natural Law and Natural Rights* (Oxford: Clarendon Press, 1980), 49.

19. Finnis, *Natural Law and Natural Rights*, 33.

20. Finnis, *Natural Law and Natural Rights*, 33/34.

21. Finnis, *Natural Law and Natural Rights*, 34.

22. Finnis, *Natural Law and Natural Rights*, 102/103.

23. John Rawls, *A Theory of Justice* (Cambridge, MA: The Belknap Press of Harvard University Press, 1971), 24.

24. See, for example, Grisez 1983, Chapell 1995, Murphy 2001, Gomez-Lobo 2002, Crowe 2019.

25. Mark Murphy, "The Natural Law Tradition in Ethics," *The Stanford Encyclopedia of Philosophy* (Summer 2019 Edition), Edward N. Zalta (ed.), https://plato.stanford.edu/archives/sum2019/entries/natural-law-ethics/.

26. A. P. d'Entrèves, *Natural Law: An Introduction to Legal Philosophy* (London: Hutchinson and Co. (Publishers) Ltd., 1951), 60.

27. d'Entrèves, *Natural Law*, 59.

28. d'Entrèves, *Natural Law*, 64.

29. d'Entrèves, *Natural Law*, 70.

30. d'Entrèves, *Natural Law*, 71.

31. d'Entrèves, *Natural Law*, 52.

32. d'Entrèves, *Natural Law*, 57/58.

33. d'Entrèves, *Natural Law*, 12.

34. d'Entrèves, *Natural Law*, 12.

35. d'Entrèves, *Natural Law*, 61.

36. Leo Strauss, *Natural Right and History* (Chicago: Chicago University Press, 1950).

37. Leo Strauss, *Natural Right and History* (Chicago: Chicago University Press, 1950), 2.

38. Leo Strauss, *The Political Philosophy of Hobbes, Its Basis and Genesis*, transl. Elsa M. Sinclair, [1936] (Chicago: Chicago University Press, 1952, Midway reprint 1984), 155/156.

39. Strauss, *Natural Right and History*, 165.

40. Jeremy Waldron, "The Role of Rights in Practical Reasoning: 'Rights' versus 'Needs,'" *The Journal of Ethics* 4 (2000): 119.

Chapter 3

Does Hobbes Rather than Locke Provide a Forerunner to Modern Theories of Rights?

THE RIGHTS THEORIES OF HOBBES AND LOCKE AS WRITTEN IN HISTORY

As I have already mentioned in the first two chapters, the history of rights theory has framed Locke as the theorist who produces the forerunner of those theories of natural rights that were to dominate, both philosophically and politically, for the next 150 years and which provided a significant part of the justification for at least two revolutions, in France and America.[1] Furthermore, Locke's political theory is seen as setting the agenda for liberal political philosophy into the modern age and his pronouncements on the rights of the individual, being central to that theory, are similarly seen as having provided the blueprint for modern theories of individual rights and particularly of the rights of the individual against the state.[2]

Locke was not the first to explore these themes, of course, and, as I outlined in Chapter One, rights theory has a long history stretching back to the middle ages. Historical scholarship has traced elements of Locke's theory back to those of William of Ockham, Gerson, Suarez, Grotius, Pufendorf, Selden and others including Hobbes,[3] but it is Locke's work that stands out as being the most widely known, widely read and in that sense also, the most influential on later thinking about individual rights. Jeremy Waldron says, in his collection of essays on liberal rights, that he is addressing the "classic tradition of liberal political theory . . . the tradition of thinkers like John Locke and John Stuart Mill,"[4] illustrating the importance of Locke's position in that tradition and how he is seen as providing a template for modern theories of rights.

The perceived position of Thomas Hobbes in the history of rights theory, could not be more different. The received view (within Hobbes scholarship as well as more broadly) is that Hobbes does not hold a theory of substantive individual rights. Indeed, individuals within a Hobbesian commonwealth are often seen as having given up all their rights to the sovereign.[5] Or, if they are acknowledged as retaining any, the retained rights are said to be weakened so much by the power and rights of the sovereign as to be rendered insignificant; rights in name only.[6] A more sophisticated argument within Hobbes scholarship, states that Hobbesian rights are all Hohfeldian liberty rights or privileges and so give rise to no corresponding duties, either in the sovereign or in other individuals.[7] Without the protections afforded by such duties, again the rights are said to be rights in name only and to provide nothing in the way of protection for their bearers. I argue, against this established orthodoxy, that Hobbes does hold a strong theory of individual rights.[8] A slew of important rights for individuals are retained into the commonwealth and held even against the sovereign. Hobbes also provides for the protection of some rights; by imposing duties on fellow subjects under the second law of nature and with the duties of the office of the sovereign, to protect the people and to encode and enforce the laws of nature. So, it is also the case that not all Hobbesian rights are mere Hohfeldian liberties or privileges.

The view I have been referring to, that Hobbes's theory of rights fails at a fundamental level, while Locke's successfully inaugurates the modern notion of liberal rights is captured in the following passage by Brian Tierney:

> I am inclined to agree that the work of Hobbes represents an aberration from earlier ideas about natural rights and natural law, though some scholars have seen his work as derived from late medieval scholasticism. In any case, his ideas have little to do with modern ways of thinking about human rights. Hobbes's characteristic teaching was that individuals have rights, but no duty to respect the rights of others. Modern codes of human rights enumerate rights that others are bound to respect. The situation is different with Locke. His rights involve duties to others, and it is widely agreed that Locke's work was an important influence in the formation of modern liberal ideas, including ideas concerning rights.[9]

Hobbes's position in the history of rights theory, however, is not a straightforward one. It is ironic perhaps that it is the historians of political thought who tend to see Hobbes as being an important thinker on the subject of rights or to have marked a significant departure in rights theory, rather than Hobbes scholars, the vast majority of whom believe that he has nothing of much significance to say on the subject of rights.[10] Leo Strauss is an example of someone who straddles both areas of scholarship and in his justly famous book, *The Political Philosophy of Hobbes: its Basis and Genesis,* he argues that Hobbes was the first to place the rights of the individual at the centre of political theory and before the obligations held under the laws of nature.[11] There is a strand of scholarship, influenced by Strauss, that picks out both Hobbes and Locke as having made a break with their conceptions of rights, that moved the notion of a right away from the strictures of natural law,[12] and this ties in with a complex debate about the move from the notion of objective natural right to subjective natural right.

What is relatively undisputed is that both Hobbes and Locke represent the "new" subjective way of understanding the term right. Both clearly talk of rights as subjective, but as above, Locke is generally heralded as the one who acknowledges the existence of duties, correlative to the rights, particularly on the part of the state, giving precedence to the rights of the individual over those of the state. I will make the case that it is more profitable to look to Hobbes than to Locke when tracing the philosophical origins of modern and current rights theory, particularly where the theories address the foundations of rights, but to do so I must first outline the argument that Hobbes does put in place duties to protect the rights that subjects hold in a Hobbesian commonwealth. This will provide the first part of the argument, that Hobbes's theory of rights is worthy of comparison to Locke's.

HOBBESIAN RIGHTS AND DUTIES

In defining the second law of nature, Hobbes states that if we are to move from the state of nature to a state of peace, we must give up all those harmful, invasive rights that we hold under the aggregate right of nature, according to which "every man has a Right to every thing: even to one another's body."[13]

> That a man be willing, when others are so too, as farre-forth, as for Peace, and defence of himself he shall think it necessary, to lay down this right to all things; and be contented with so much liberty against other men, as he would allow other men against himself.[14]

He goes on,

> . . . To lay down a mans Right to any thing, is to devest himself of the Liberty, of hindering another of the benefit of his own Right to the same. For he that renounceth, or passeth away his Right, giveth not to any other man a Right which he had not before; because there is nothing to which every man had not Right by Nature: but only **standeth out of his way, that he may enjoy his own original Right, without hindrance from him**. (My emphasis in bold.)[15]

Further,

> And when a man hath . . . abandoned or granted away his Right; then is he
> said to be OBLIGED or BOUND, not to hinder those, to whom such Right is
> granted, or abandoned, from the benefit of it: and that he Ought and it is his
> DUTY, not to make void that voluntary act of his own.[16]

Hobbes is saying that individuals, when they give up the "right to all
things" of the right of nature, will, for each invasive right they give up, take
on a correlative duty to respect the corresponding right. For example, if I give
up my right to your body, that is, my right to invade or violate your body,
which I hold under the right of nature, then I take on a duty to respect your
right to your own body, which includes your right to bodily integrity. Hobbes
is saying that when we all agree, under the second law of nature, to renounce
or transfer our invasive rights to each other, we also agree to take on duties
to stand out of the way of each other's exercise of our own, retained rights.
As above, when we all give up our rights to (invade) each other's bodies,
we take on duties to respect each other's rights to our own bodies. After this
process is complete, I have a right to my own body, which includes a right
to my own bodily integrity, to my complete (un-invaded, un-attacked) body,
that is correlated with the duty of all others to respect my right to my body,
or not to stand in the way of my exercising my right.

In other words, we could say, in Hohfeldian terms, that I now have a claim
right to my body and to bodily integrity that is correlated with the duty of all
others to respect that right. I have reasons for preferring not to use a Hohfeldian
analysis but with this example it is possible to say that what Hobbes describes
as taking place under the second law of nature is a process by which invasive rights are given up, and duties are taken on to respect the non-invasive,
retained rights, thereby transforming those retained liberty rights into claim
rights. (A complication arises when one considers that the retained rights are
still liberties, because all rights are liberties for Hobbes. Now, there is no
problem in my view, with having liberties (or freedoms) that become protected by correlative duties and therefore in Hohfeldian terms become claim
rights, but for Hohfeld, a liberty is a right without correlated duties, so we run
into difficulties with Hohfeld's definitions if we use his analysis).

Furthermore, once a sovereign is instituted and we are in a commonwealth
it will be the duty of the sovereign to make these rights and duties a matter of
law and to enforce the law.

> . . . the Lawes of Nature, . . . in the condition of mere Nature . . . are not prop-
> erly Lawes, but qualities that dispose men to peace, and to obedience. When a
> Common-wealth is once settled, then are they actually Lawes, and not before;

as being the commands of the common-wealth; and therefore also Civil Lawes: For it is the Sovereign Power that obliges men to obey them.[17]

So, there are duties that are correlated with Hobbesian rights and these will be encoded into law and enforced by the sovereign. We have then, in Hobbes's theory, important retained rights with duties to respect those rights that will also, eventually, be enforced by law. That is a brief rehearsal of an argument that Hobbes does provide some rights for Hobbesian subjects that have corresponding duties and enough at least to show that there is plenty of textual evidence to support such an argument.

RIGHTS IN LOCKE'S THEORY

There has been a debate amongst Locke scholars that is still on going, about whether or not we are justified in trying to detach his theory of rights and his political theory more generally, from its theological premises. I shall address A. J. Simmons' important contribution to this debate below and argue, against him, that it is not credible to detach Lockean arguments from their theological wellspring. Locke makes it clear from the start of the *Second Treatise* that rights for individuals are granted, defined, and governed by natural law. A person "may not, unless it be to do justice on an offender, take away, or impair the life, or what tends to the preservation of the life, the liberty, health, limb or goods of another." He continues, "And that all men may be restrained from invading others rights, and from doing hurt to one another, and the law of nature be observed."[18] It is worth just noting that Locke has introduced the notion of rights here by describing duties held under the law of nature, and those duties towards individuals prescribe what rights they have. Locke also makes clear that he supports the view that all of mankind is born into a state in which the law of nature and the rights he refers to are already in existence, as he says, "Man being born, as has been proved, with a title to perfect freedom, and an uncontrolled enjoyment of all the rights and privileges of the law of nature."[19] So, for Locke, the notion and existence of rights held by individuals is thoroughly dependent upon an independently existing natural law and on God as the source of that law.

One question to be addressed then is this: can his theory of rights be salvaged if we take away the theological premises? This question has been answered in the affirmative by A. J. Simmons in his book, *The Lockean Theory of Rights*,[20] and I will examine some of his arguments below. Commentators have sometimes taken the view or at least suggested as a possibility that we can "bracket out" the theology and we are then left with a seemingly modern moral law that says we are all equal and should not invade each other's rights. As Waldron says, "the belief that some such bracketing must be possible . . . this hope is crucial for modern secular liberalism."[21] He has addressed this question recently in his book on Lockean equality,[22] but he makes a strikingly different and very interesting argument that raises a third possibility, that the theological arguments are actually better than the secular ones. So, he argues that far from "bracketing out" the theological arguments, we should leave them in, examine them and recognize how good they are. I don't think his argument can work in the end, because in my view it is not plausible to make an argument that relies on theological premises, to a general philosophical audience in the twenty-first century in the West. The problem, simply put, is that the theological premises will be rejected by a large portion of that audience and therefore any argument that follows from them will be similarly rejected.

John Dunn says, in his seminal 1969 work on Locke's theory,[23] "I have argued throughout that a defensible theology is a necessary condition for the cogency of many of his arguments and that there is every reason to believe that Locke himself would have assented to this judgement."[24] Simmons makes an interesting case for seeing Locke's theory of rights as containing within it "strains" of Kantian thinking as well as traditional natural law thinking and argues that Locke's theory can be "reconstructed" along Kantian lines in such a way that it "speaks to" modern rights theories. I argue that Simmons does not succeed or at least does not succeed in ways that would weaken the case I am making, that we should look to Hobbes rather than Locke, as providing a precursor to modern theories of rights that "speaks to" current rights theories.

Simmons starts by acknowledging the dependence on theological premises of Locke's theory, specifically of his moral theory. He categorizes Locke's theory of natural law as a command theory, defining a law as "the decree of a superior will" which lays down "what is and is not to be done."[25] As God's creation, Locke argues, according to Simmons, that we are subject to His will. And he drives the point home in *An Essay Concerning Human Understanding* when he says that without knowledge of God and God's will, the atheist "can never be certain that anything is his duty."[26] So, Simmons argues that Locke's moral theory, that is, his theory of natural law and natural rights, is given its (moral) authority by God and that moral obligation is generated by God's will and nothing else. Despite this strong endorsement of the view of Locke's theory as thoroughly dependent on theology, Simmons argues that it is possible to reconstruct the theory without the theological premises. He characterizes Locke's moral theory as "pluralistic at a variety of levels,"

> First, it is a theory that is neither right-based, nor duty-based, nor virtue-based, but . . . takes seriously all three categories. Second, within the deontic portion of the theory, it appeals to both consequentialist and deontological considerations to justify the rights and duties it defends. And finally, it is pluralistic in that

at the foundations of the theory arguments proceed from both theological and secular starting points.[27]

As I am concerned with the foundations of the theory, rather than with the specific rights and duties it gives rise to, I will address only those arguments concerning that aspect of it. Simmons sets out the argument more tentatively than one might expect given the strong claim he is making. He says we can "occasionally . . . see a hint of a different position at work in Locke's arguments, a position more amenable to intellectualism and to the secular moral theories of the Enlightenment than to the dominant strain of voluntarism in Locke."[28] And he adds, "it may sometimes seem as if Locke agrees with Kant."[29] To support the claim, he refers to Locke's quotation of a passage from Hooker, in which passage, according to Simmons, Hooker derives our moral obligations from human equality. The quoted passage begins, "[t]he like natural inducement, hath brought men to know that it is no less their duty, to love others than themselves, for seeing those things which are equal, must needs all have one measure"; And the passage ends,

> My desire therefore to be loved of my equals in nature, as much as possible may be, imposeth upon me a natural duty of bearing to themward, fully the like affection; From which relation of equality between our selves and them, that are as our selves, what several rules and cannons, natural reason both drawn for direction of life, no man is ignorant.[30]

This passage establishes, according to Simmons, that "the duties of natural law are derived, without reference to God's will or His commands, from the fact that "those things which are equal, must needs all have one measure."[31] And Simmons continues, "the argument strongly suggests that it is the irrationality (or inconsistency) of treating others as if they were different from ourselves that establishes its immorality. There is a kind of "practical contradiction" involved in harmful conduct towards others."[32] This certainly sounds Kantian and Simmons argues exactly that; he says there is a strong similarity between the second formulation of Kant's Categorical Imperative and what he calls "the Hooker-Locke argument." He points out that Locke, like Kant, says that we are not "made for one another's uses."[33] We must treat others like the persons that they are, because to do otherwise would be irrational. Simmons adds this to the theological element of Locke's theory. "Just as we must for Locke respect God's property, whether in ourselves or others, the Kantian strain in Locke requires us to respect humanity (personhood), whether in ourselves or others."[34]

Simmons does succeed, I think, in pointing to a Kantian "strain" in some of Locke's thinking on morality and this is valuable and interesting but the question I want to address here is the much more narrow one of whether he succeeds in showing that we can successfully reconstruct Locke's theory without the theological premises. He seems to undermine his own argument (and the claim, as above, that the theory is pluralistic at its foundations with arguments starting from both theological and secular starting points) in the following ways. First, he says that he is not suggesting that his argument is "unproblematic" or that it is "especially central in Locke's thought." He is, he says, only pointing to a "certain affinity between one strand of Locke's argument and one kind of Kantian position."[35] Second, he says that the "most obvious affinities between the Lockean and Kantian theories, however, are not here at the foundations of the theories, where the Kantian must argue for a ground of obligation that Locke would never have acknowledged as the sole ground," but rather, the obvious similarities are "in the contents of the moral theories flowing from these foundations."[36] Third, Simmons does not believe that Kantian theories are fully consistent with the "spirit" of Locke's moral theory, indeed such a claim would, he says, "be misleading." He goes on, "God is too much at the centre of Locke's work for such secular, Kantian arguments to capture its essence."[37] Furthermore, Locke emphasizes "throughout his work that only God's will can make actions obligatory."[38]

These careful provisos given by Simmons ensure that he is not claiming too much for Locke or ignoring the evidence of the importance and centrality of the theological premises, and they make for a nuanced reading of Locke, allowing him to explore the similarities in the content of the rights and duties Locke argues for and those generated by a Kantian theory. The arguments about the similarity in the content of the moral rights and duties generated by different moral theories, however, do not help to establish anything about the foundations of those theories or the premises they rely on. Moral theories starting from utterly different premises and relying on incompatible notions of what morality consists in, often give rise to similar content in terms of the actions they promote or forbid. Similarly, the recognition of some arguments and references in the theory which appear Kantian in their reasoning or approach, will not provide any kind of challenge to Locke's primary moral argument, which is theological.

If, as above, Locke argues that only God's will can make actions obligatory, then nothing else can make actions obligatory for Locke and so if we take out of Locke's moral theory, the premise of God's existence and His intentions for us and His will, then we are left without anything that can generate genuine moral obligation. Rationality may provide additional reasons for treating others as ourselves but it is not, on its own, going to oblige us to do so, so we cannot substitute a Kantian deontology for Locke's natural law.

Similarly, we will not be able to substitute any form of utilitarianism, including rule utilitarianism. This brings me to the other argument Simmons offers for his claim that Locke's moral theory is pluralistic at its foundations and has arguments proceeding from both theological and secular starting points (as above). This is the argument that, what Simmons calls, the "superstructure" of Locke's theory is rule-consequentialist.

> The superstructure of Locke's moral theory, then, is a kind of rule-consequentialism, with the preservation of mankind serving as the 'ultimate end' to be advanced. The fundamental law specifies this end, and all of the specific rules of natural law are members of that set of rules obedience to which best promotes the preservation of mankind.[39]

I find this argument rather baffling. Simmons argues that a rule consequentialist superstructure will "fit" Locke's theory better than an act-consequentialist one. But why suggest that the theory is consequentialist at all? He has explained that what he is doing in the section on "superstructure" is showing how some of Locke's arguments, rather than appealing directly to God's will, appeal to it "indirectly by rule-consequentialist reasoning."[40] But if the ultimate source of the obligation and of the fundamental law itself, is, according to Locke, God's will, then in what sense is the (moral) reasoning rule-consequentialist? Rather, for Locke it must be one of God's commands that we should act so as to promote the preservation of mankind. Or, if not a direct command it must be a law we can reason to from His intentions. If it is not and is just a law that we have created in order to further the 'good' (as we see it) of the preservation of mankind, then surely for Locke it cannot be a moral law?

Again, what I need for my argument is just a demonstration of what Simmons has demonstrated very adequately himself; namely, that Locke's theory of rights (as part of his moral theory) is generated by his theory of natural law, which in turn relies on theological premises that include the premise that moral obligation comes only from God's will, that a law is "the decree of a superior will" which "binds men,"[41] and that "the taking away of God, though but even in thought, dissolves all."[42] This is enough for an argument that Locke's theory, while it may contain "strains" of other kinds of moral thinking, including Kantian thinking and that it may even contain or refer to arguments which seem to find other ways of generating morality, cannot nevertheless, be detached from its theological premises without "dissolving all." In other words, Locke's moral theory depends solely on its theological premises to provide the source of moral duties and rights and of moral obligation itself.

That is the strong argument against looking to Locke as providing a fore-runner of modern and current rights theories. There is also a weaker argu-ment; that even if it is possible to adapt Locke's theory so that it is compatible with modern and current theories to the extent that it makes sense to look to it as a forerunner of those theories, we have, with Hobbes, a theory of rights, that without any adaptation or "reconstruction" is arguably already a mod-ern, secular theory of rights, or it is certainly plausible to read it as such and therefore there is a much stronger case for looking to Hobbes as providing a forerunner to modern and current rights theories.

There is not the space here to discuss the details of other arguments within Locke scholarship, for example, arguments that Locke is not a voluntarist after all but rather is an intellectualist on natural law and so we do not have to look to God's will but only to our own reason for the content and author-ity of natural law. Many of these arguments explore apparently contradictory statements by Locke, particularly between his epistemological writing and his political writing. Similarly, there is not space to explore in more detail the Straussian notion that Locke's theological commitments are not sincere but, as with many other writers of the period, put in in order to protect them from persecution. On the balance of probabilities, it seems to me that the weight of evidence supports both the sincerity of Locke's theological commitments and the prevailing view that he is a voluntarist.

RIGHTS IN HOBBES'S THEORY

How does Hobbes establish his notion of individual rights? Having described the state of nature as a state of (civil) war of each against each, where self-preservation is the only priority, and having introduced the notion that by our reason we can arrive at laws of nature which are rules "by which a man is forbidden to do, that which is destructive of his life, or taketh away the means of so preserving the same; and to omit, that, by which he thinketh it may be best preserved,."[43] he goes on to develop the notion of the right of nature and then to set out what sort of rights we should give up and what sort of rights we should hold on to. What is important for my argument here is the philosophical account of rights that Hobbes provides. What is the foun-dational notion for a right? What premises does he rely on to formulate his theory of rights?

The foundational notion for a right is clear; it is liberty. Hobbes's definition of liberty in Chapter 14 of *Leviathan* as, "the absence of external impedi-ments,"[44] is controversial however. It is infamously restrictive. There is much debate about how Hobbes's understanding of liberty should be interpreted and I will not enter that debate here but will simply state that I follow Michael

Goldsmith and others in reading Hobbesian liberty as including freedom from legal and moral constraints as well as from physical restraints, drawing on Hobbes's remarks on liberty in Chapter 21 of *Leviathan* and elsewhere.[45]

So, we have a foundational notion of liberty to ground that of a right and this may be liberty in the sense of physical freedom to act or forbear from acting, or the freedom to act or forbear from acting in the sense of freedom from legal or moral constraints. What premises does Hobbes rely on to arrive at his notion of a right? There are no theological premises that are obvious. There is no straightforward reference, as there is in Locke's theory, to God's intentions in our creation or to natural law with God as its source. Hobbes gives us, in the early chapters of *Leviathan*, a famously mechanical, materialist description of persons as driven by desires and fears, which desires and fears lead us into a state of war of each against each. But the same desires and fears, when joined with the ability to make rational decisions, lead to our creation of a set of rational principles which will help us to preserve ourselves and to live a peaceful and commodious life, that is, to the laws of nature.

So, with Hobbes, we seem to have only premises about human characteristics that are empirically verifiable or observable and some assumptions about our ability to make rational choices and to predict the outcome of our actions with some accuracy. There is also an old question within Hobbes scholarship, hanging over the status and composition of the laws of nature and this is inextricably linked to the vexed question of Hobbes's moral theory. There has been a longstanding debate about this with those on one side arguing that it is a subjectivist theory, with claims that it proposes, for example, ethical egoism, or rule egoism,[46] and those on the other side arguing that it is an objectivist deontology, with claims that it proposes, for example, a natural law theory or a Kantian deontology.[47] The various, seemingly contradictory or inconsistent remarks Hobbes makes about the laws of nature provide endless material for this debate. One small example is Hobbes's remark that "The Lawes of Nature are Immutable and Eternall."[48] This sounds as though he is endorsing a traditional notion of natural law, until one reads on "For Injustice, Ingratitude, Arrogance, Pride, Iniquity, Acception of person, and the rest, can never be made lawful. For it can never be that Warre shall preserve life, and Peace destroy it."[49] And we are, arguably, back to the argument that the laws of nature are rational precepts required for preservation. There are many more examples. The aspect of this debate that is of relevance here is the importance of remarks Hobbes makes about God in relation to the status of the laws of nature. At the end of Chapter 15, in a passage that has caused great confusion and discussion, Hobbes says,

> These dictates of Reason, men use to call by the name of Lawes; but improperly:
> for they are but Conclusions, or Theorems concerning what conduceth to the

conservation and defence of themselves; whereas Law, properly is the word of him, that by right hath command over others. But yet if we consider the same Theorems, as delivered in the word of God, that by right commandeth all things; then are they properly called Lawes.[50]

This raises the issue of whether God has a place in Hobbes's political theory and if so whether the theory of rights has a theological premise. If we look at the structure of the language used in the passage, we can see that the last sentence is conditional. If, we consider the laws of nature, as delivered in the word of God . . . then they are properly called Laws. The first sentence, on the other hand, is declarative. The laws of nature are but conclusions or theorems . . . that are conducive to our conservation and defence. So, Hobbes is saying that the laws of nature are conclusions or theorems, or as he has said previously, "general rules" for our conservation and defence and if we were to consider them as delivered in the word of God, then we could quite properly call them laws. The reason he puts it this way of course is that Hobbes holds a command theory of law and so nothing in his view can properly be called a law unless it is the command of a sovereign. The second sentence of the passage, which brings God into the discussion, is generally seen as ambiguous and confusing, at least in part because of the conditional language. It is a hypothetical proposition and it is unclear how much weight we should attach to it. For my purposes, what matters is whether it creates a theological premise that Hobbes relies on for his theory of rights. I support the widely accepted view that, as J. C. A. Gaskin puts it, what "distinguishes Hobbes's laws of nature from the traditional laws of nature is that Hobbes's precepts are, at the start, independent of the will of God."[51] Then, if we interpret the passage above as meaning that Hobbes says that the laws of nature do happen to tally with those laws given by God, then we can also agree with Gaskin that, "They do not need to be justified by the external authority of God, although in fact they have such authority."[52]

If God is not necessarily involved in our conceiving of the laws of nature, do we still have reason, according to Hobbes, to comply with them? The answer is clearly yes, because they can still function as maxims or rules for our preservation. So, in this context, it doesn't really matter if Hobbes is putting forward God as the one who makes the laws of nature into proper moral laws rather than just theorems or maxims for preservation. Without God, we can argue that Hobbes is still providing a political or prudential argument about which rights we should give up, which we should hold onto and which we should protect. We should still give up those invasive liberties under the second law of nature and we should still take on the duties to respect those rights in each other. Hobbes has an argument with or without God, that individuals need to make these rules and comply with them in order to best preserve themselves and to be able to live a commodious life. And the rights, the liberties, are still there with or without God because there is no theological premise concerning the state of liberty that individuals are in when in a state of nature. Hobbes gives no role to God in his description of the state of nature or the right of nature. One could say rather that, in the context of the time, He is conspicuous by His absence.

One of the strikingly modern aspects of Hobbes's theory is that it provides pragmatic, political arguments that are independent of any God given moral commands or indeed of any particular moral theory. Some might object that this is to speak too loosely, for any political theory must have as its basis a theory of political morality but it is certainly possible to argue, in Hobbes's case, that the values he picks out as all important for his political argument, include peace and the freedom to live a commodious life and self-preservation but do not presuppose a theology or the existence of a moral law that exists in some way prior to or independently of human society.

There is another passage that commentators might wish to point to, in making the argument that God is a necessary part of the laws of nature and therefore of Hobbes's moral theory. This is the passage in Chapter 32 of *Leviathan*, where Hobbes says,

> . . . we are not to renounce our Senses, and Experience; nor (that which is the undoubted Word of God) our natural Reason. For they are the talents which he hath put into our hands to negotiate, till the coming again of our blessed Saviour; and therefore not to be folded up in the Napkin of an Implicate Faith, but employed in the purchase of Justice, Peace, and true Religion.[53]

In this passage Hobbes is stressing the theological beliefs appropriate to a Christian standpoint; not surprisingly perhaps, this is, after all, the first page of Part III of *Leviathan*, "Of a Christian Commonwealth." But in the passage previous to this, the one with which he starts this new section, he says,

> I have derived the Rights of Soveraigne Power, and the duty of Subjects hitherto, from the Principles of Nature onely; such as Experience has found true, or Consent (concerning the use of words) has made so; that is to say, from the nature of Men, known to us by Experience, and from Definitions (of such words as are Essential to all Political reasoning) universally agreed on.[54]

The point he is making here is that up to this point he has relied only on human experience and human language to make his arguments and develop his political theory. And we should remind ourselves that "up to this point" includes Chapters 1–31, that is, "Part I, Of Man."[55] and "Part II, Of Commonwealth."[56] In other words, he has set out the entire political theory before this point and without inserting unambiguous theological premises. I argue that Hobbes has provided convincing, pragmatic or prudential reasons for conforming to the laws of nature and transferring and renouncing our invasive rights and taking on duties to respect retained rights, without having to appeal to any conventional theory of morality or to God as author or source of that morality. So, whether Hobbes believes that God is the source of moral authority or not, does not matter, in terms of the theory he is proposing. His arguments will work without any theology. And whatever way one reads Hobbes's moral theory, it will still provide arguments for the political order he recommends.

The foundations of subjects' rights and duties can lie either in the purely pragmatic arguments Hobbes gives us, concerning what is necessary for us to best preserve ourselves, or in an appeal to moral arguments that may or may not include God as the source and authority of the moral law. To those commentators who argue that it is only the sovereign's ultimate duty to God (and by implication to obey the God-given laws of nature), that provides the binding authority of the laws of nature, I would simply reply that the laws of nature would still bind as human laws, commanded by a sovereign and subjects would still have more than enough reasons to obey those laws. And if the sovereign failed to encode and enforce the laws of nature (in failing to do his duty to God), then, as the sovereign would be failing in his primary duty of ensuring the safety of the people, subjects would be free to turn elsewhere for their protection.[57] Presumably they would turn to someone (or some assembly) who would be able to encode and enforce their rights and duties.

My argument is that Hobbes's theory of rights is constructed in such a way that it is not dependent on theological premises. I am happy to leave it as an open question whether or not God is, for Hobbes, crucial as the author of and/ or the source of obligation concerning the laws of nature, that is, the moral theory, as this is a subject of continued scholarly dispute. The important point for my argument is that a reader coming to Hobbes's theory of rights in the twenty-first century can consider the arguments without confronting premises that would, for many, rule it out as a plausible theory. This immediately gives it much in common with modern rights theories, including modern natural rights theories such as that of John Finnis, who argues that his version of natural law theory is not dependent on theological premises.

RELATIONSHIP TO MODERN RIGHTS THEORIES

If I have succeeded in establishing that Hobbes proposes a theory of rights in *Leviathan*,[58] which is not reliant on any theological premises and that Locke's theory of rights is thoroughly dependent on such premises, even if it is possible to reconstruct parts of the theory without them, then this gives me my first argument. On this ground alone we can say that Hobbes's theory has far more in common with modern and current theories of rights than does Locke's theory. After all, modern theories of rights were largely forged in the aftermath of the criticisms of Hume, Bentham, and others and of the resulting discrediting of theories of natural rights. The project of most rights theorists since that time has been to ground and justify rights without recourse to the theology or metaphysics of traditional natural law theory.

My argument also demonstrates that there is a theory of rights that was already in existence when Locke wrote the *Two Treatises*, which circumvents the philosophical problems that arose from Locke's reliance on theological premises. I have briefly rehearsed an argument that Hobbes's theory is a theory of substantive rights for individuals which also provides for the protection of certain important rights by corresponding duties. This provides an argument that, contrary to the views of many commentators, Hobbes's theory of rights is strong enough to compete with Locke's and to be recognized as a significant theory of rights. Even if this part of my argument is not accepted, and I have only been able to sketch it briefly, it is not necessary for the next part of my argument, which concerns his approach to theorizing rights rather than his contribution to normative discussions of rights within political theory.

I argue that the way Hobbes structures his discussions of rights and the approach he takes particularly at the start of his discussion of rights in *Leviathan*, gives his theory far more in common with modern rights theories within analytic philosophy and jurisprudence, than that of Locke's much more loosely structured theory. To start with a very simple yet important point; Hobbes defines a right. He tells us very clearly, in Chapter 14 of *Leviathan*, exactly what a right is and he defines the term right in relation to law, to obligation and to the right of nature. So, having defined a right as a liberty he says,

> For though they that speak of this subject, use to confound Jus, and Lex, Right and Law; yet they ought to be distinguished; because RIGHT, consisteth in liberty to do, or to forbear; Whereas LAW, determineth, and bindeth to one of them: so that Law and Right, differ as much, as Obligation, and Liberty; which in one and the same matter are inconsistent.[59]

And he has already made clear two paragraphs earlier that,

> The RIGHT OF NATURE, which Writers commonly call Jus Naturale, is the Liberty each man hath, to use his own power, as he will himself, for the preservation of his own Nature; that is to say, of his own Life; and consequently, of

doing any thing, which in his own Judgement and Reason, hee shall conceive to be the aptest means thereunto.[60]

Hobbes has given us a wealth of information in these passages about his understanding of what a right is, how rights arise, the foundational notion for a right, and its relation to other important notions such as law and obligation. The latter is particularly useful as he makes it clear that he sees a right as in some sense opposed to an obligation or contradictory to the notion of obligation or simply as being free of obligation and that he understands the contrast between law and right as being the contrast between being bound to a particular action or omission and being free to choose an action or omission. This contrasts sharply with the notion of a right as just the other side of a duty which Locke gives in some places and which is common in discussions of rights generally.

Hobbes's clear definition of a right as a liberty and his statements explaining the notion of a right in relation to other closely related notions, gives us a conceptual framework with which to explore the theory of rights he is expounding. His exposition of the right of nature followed by the explanation of how the right to every thing must be curtailed, demonstrates that while all rights are liberties not all liberties are rights, or at least not rights that we can justify holding onto if we are to live in society. As he remarks in the *Elements of Law*, "[b]ut that right of all men to all things, is in effect no better than if no man had right to any thing. For there is little use and benefit of the right a man hath, when another as strong, or stronger than himself hath right to the same."[61]

This is what leads to war, as he goes on, "whereby one man invadeth with right, and another with right resisteth; . . . the estate of men in this natural liberty is the estate of war."[62] And so, while recognizing that Hobbes calls all these liberties rights, he is making clear and we can certainly argue, that it is only those liberties we are justified in holding onto that are rights in the sense we might understand the term as referring to moral or political rights. So, a moral or political right, for Hobbes, is a liberty that individuals are justified in holding within civil society. He develops his theory of rights to include: invasive rights, held in the state of nature, that must be given up, rights necessary for preservation to be held onto, and some extensive rights also held onto that are necessary not just to physically survive but to "live well" or to be able to live life "so as not to be weary of it." And all of these rights can be understood within the definition of a right as a liberty.[63]

Locke, on the other hand, provides no definition of a right. As Simmons says "Locke . . . offers no definition of a 'right' generally, nor does he ever say clearly what a right is."[64] Simmons then suggests that "[w]e know that rights are 'freedoms' of a sort and that the central rights in Locke are the logical correlates of others' duties (and so are protected freedoms)."[65] He goes on to conclude that the notions of claim and entitlement probably "best fit(s) the way Locke talks about rights,"[66] but says that it is not possible to characterize Locke's theory as either a choice or will theory of rights or a benefit or interest theory. Rather, we should think that, for Locke, "both choice and benefit are central to the idea of right."[67]

Locke sometimes uses right and duty interchangeably and he uses "right" in other ways as well. He uses the term to cover at least the following: claim, entitlement, "title," a property, dominion and freedom/liberty (although he also refers to "a right to resume their original liberty" implying a distinction between the two terms).[68] Locke's relatively loose way of talking about rights makes it hard to pin down exactly what he means by a right and how he would analyse the notion of a right in relation to other important related notions such as, duty, law and obligation.

Hobbes's approach to the subject of rights can best be described as "analytical." While Locke's theory says a great deal about the rights of individuals within a political order, in the context of a normative discussion, it does not, I argue, help us to analyse any more clearly what it means to say that someone has a right or how the notion of a right can be distinguished from other important moral and political values or concepts. In other words, it does not help us to engage with the sort of philosophical analysis of rights that we find in discussions of modern and current rights theory and particularly in jurisprudential discussions of rights theory. And because Hobbes's approach could be said to "match" that of modern rights theorists, or to illustrate that he is engaged in the same "project," I argue that in this sense we can say that Hobbes's theory of rights can be seen as a forerunner to modern and current rights theories. His theory stands out from Locke's in this regard and it is Hobbes rather than Locke who analyses rights in this very modern way, who undertakes a conceptual analysis of rights that seeks to define and understand what it is to say that individuals have rights and who does so, without relying on any theological premises.

Relationship to Current Discussions of Rights

Hobbes's use of the notion of liberty to ground that of a right means that we can use his theory as a contribution to the debate about what works best as the grounding notion of a right. It enables us, for example, to ask whether liberty does the job better than interest or will. Where "interest" theory fails to explain interests we have that are not considered to be rights (as in the example, that I have an interest in publishing articles in academic journals but no right to do so), we can ask whether the notion of liberty would do better. We can try out the Hobbesian understanding of a right as a liberty to see if it produces as many or less (or more) counterexamples and to see if it seems to capture as much or more or less of our common understanding of a right. On the other hand, with Locke's theory, because we are not given a clear definition and because he uses the term "right" in several different ways, it would not be possible to conduct the same kind of comparative conceptual analysis. And it is just such conceptual analysis that makes Hobbes's theory of rights closer to current rights theories and to philosophical discussion of those theories, than Locke's theory. To put it another way, one could say that Hobbes's theory of rights "speaks to" current theories in a way that Locke's theory fails to do.

Locke's theory does not easily become part of current discussions of what rights are and how we might best understand them. Rather it stands, frozen in time, as an important exemplar of a type of rights theory, that is, one of natural rights based on natural law, hugely important historically and enormously influential as part of the history of liberal political thought. Yet it is a theory that in some important sense we cannot return to in current analytical investigations of the foundations and functions of rights, to seek a new insight or understanding. We know it is there and we understand the contribution it makes. We can of course, still discuss its enormous contribution to normative political thought. But if we are investigating the philosophical foundations of and justifications for rights in the twenty-first century, we cannot use a theory that fails to clearly define a right or to provide a grounding notion or analysis of a right and that is thoroughly dependent upon theological premises.

CONCLUSION

To end with Dunn's final sentences, "[w]e have, it seems, come to accept in the broadest of terms the politics of Locke but, while doing so, we have firmly discarded the reasons which alone made them seem acceptable even to Locke. It is hard to believe that this combination can be quite what we need today."[69] I would put my conclusion even more strongly. We continue to look back to Locke's theory of rights as providing the template for modern theories of rights and yet most commentators have thoroughly rejected the premises on which that theory relies. We continue to celebrate that theory as a great move forward in political thought and as establishing principles of individual rights that we hold dear today and yet we reject the reasoning that led Locke to his conclusions. On the other hand, we have failed to recognize that Hobbes's theory of rights does provide a genuine forerunner of modern and current theories of rights. And so, it is Hobbes's theory that we should look to in this context, rather than Locke's, to see how it can help in the on-going project to explain and justify, with arguments that are philosophically viable in the twenty-first century, the intuitions many of us have about the importance and inviolability of certain individual rights.

NOTES

1. As Peter Laslett puts it in his Introduction to the Two Treatises of Government, "The prime reason for the importance attached to this book of Locke's is its enormous historical influence. . . . [T]he part which it played in the growth to maturity of English liberalism, . . . in the development of those movements which had their issue in the American Revolution, the French Revolution and their parallels in southern America, in Ireland, in India." (John Locke, *Two Treatises of Government,* ed., Peter Laslett (Cambridge: Cambridge University Press, 1960), 3.

2. This chapter, from the second paragraph onwards, was first published as "An Immodest Proposal: Hobbes Rather than Locke Provides a Forerunner For Modern rights Theory," *Law and Philosophy* 32, no. 4 (July 2013): 515–538, Springer Nature.

3. See for example, Brian Tierney, "The Idea of Natural Rights-Origins and Persistence," *North Western Journal.of Human Rights* 2, no. 1 (2004): 2–12, Brian Tierney, "Historical Roots of Modern Rights: Before Locke and After," *Ave Maria Law Review* 3, no. 1 (2005): 23–43, Richard Tuck, *Natural Rights Theories: Their Origin and Development* (Cambridge: Cambridge University Press, 1979).

4. Jeremy Waldron (ed.), *Liberal Rights: Collected Papers 1981–1991* (Cambridge: Cambridge University Press, 1993), 1.

5. ". . . the subject having given up his rights cannot now appeal to them": Alan Ryan, "Hobbes's Political Philosophy," in *The Cambridge Companion to Hobbes*, ed Tom Sorell (Cambridge: Cambridge University Press, 1996), 235.

6. "No one could claim rights of self-ownership against such power," Will Kymlicka, *Contemporary Political Philosophy* (Oxford: Clarendon Press, 1990), 130.

7. See for example, David Gauthier, *The Logic of Leviathan* (Oxford: Clarendon Press, 1969), Jean Hampton, *Hobbes and the Social Contract Tradition* (Cambridge: Cambridge University Press, 1986), Gregory Kavka, *Hobbesian Moral and Political Theory* (Princeton: Princeton University Press, 1986) (though Kavka renames a liberty right as a permission right), Claire Finkelstein, "A Puzzle About Hobbes on Self-Defence," *Pacific Philosophical Quarterly* 82 no. 3–4. (2001): 332–361, Susanne Sreedhar, *Hobbes on Resistance* (New York: Cambridge University Press, 2010).

8. Eleanor Curran, *Reclaiming the Rights of the Hobbesian Subject* (Basingstoke: Palgrave Macmillan, 2007).

9. Tierney, "Historical Roots of Modern Rights: Before Locke and After."

10. Claire Finkelstein and Susanne Sreedhar, are two notable exceptions. Their recent work has drawn attention to the significance of some Hobbesian rights, although they do both also maintain that these rights are liberty rights with no correlative duties. See Finkelstein, "A Puzzle about Hobbes on Self-Defence," and Susanne Sreedhar, *Hobbes on Resistance.*

11. Leo Strauss, *The Political Philosophy of Hobbes, Its Basis and Genesis* (1936), trans. Elsa M. Sinclair (Chicago: Chicago University Press, 1952, Midway reprint 1984),

12. Tierney, "Historical Roots of Modern Rights: Before Locke and After."

13. Thomas Hobbes, *Leviathan*, ed. C. B. Macpherson (London: Penguin Books, 1968), 190.

14. Hobbes, *Leviathan*, 190.

15. Hobbes, *Leviathan*, 190–91.

16. Hobbes, *Leviathan*, 191.

17. Hobbes, *Leviathan*, 314.

18. Locke, *Second Treatise*, 9.

19. Locke, *Second Treatise*, 46 (my italics).

20. A. J. Simmons, *The Lockean Theory of Rights* (Princeton: Princeton University Press, 1992).

21. Jeremy Waldron, *God, Locke, and Equality: Christian Foundations in Locke's Political Thought* (Cambridge: Cambridge University Press, 2002), 45.

22. Waldron, *God, Locke, and Equality*, 45.

23. John Dunn, *The Political Thought of John Locke: An Historical Account of the 'Two Treatises of Government'* (Cambridge: Cambridge University Press, 1969).

24. Dunn, *The Political Thought of John Locke*, 263.

25. A. John Simmons, *The Lockean Theory of Rights* (Princeton: Princeton University Press, 1992), 22, quoting Locke's Essays on the Law of Nature, 111–113.

26. Simmons, *The Lockean Theory of Rights*, 39, quoting Locke's Essay on Human Understanding, 1.2.13.

27. Simmons, *The Lockean Theory of Rights*, 11.

28. Simmons, *The Lockean Theory of Rights*, 39.

29. Simmons, *The Lockean Theory of Rights*, 40.

30. Simmons, *The Lockean Theory of Rights*, quoting Richard Hooker, Ecclesiastical Polity, Book 1. (II, 5).

31. Simmons, *The Lockean Theory of Rights*, 41.

32. Simmons, *The Lockean Theory of Rights*, 41.

33. Simmons, *The Lockean Theory of Rights*, 9.

34. Simmons, *The Lockean Theory of Rights*, 42.

35. Simmons, *The Lockean Theory of Rights*, 42.

36. Simmons, *The Lockean Theory of Rights*, 42–43.

37. Simmons, *The Lockean Theory of Rights*, 44.

38. Simmons, *The Lockean Theory of Rights*, 45.

39. Simmons, *The Lockean Theory of Rights*, 50–51.

40. Simmons, *The Lockean Theory of Rights*, 45.

41. Simmons, *The Lockean Theory of Rights*, 22.

42. Simmons, *The Lockean Theory of Rights*, 39, quoting Locke's Letter Concerning Toleration, 156.

43. Hobbes, *Leviathan*, 189.

44. Hobbes, *Leviathan*, 189.

45. "But as men, for the attaining of peace, and conservation of themselves thereby, have made an Artificial Man, which we call a Common-wealth; so also have they made Artificial Chains, called Civil Lawes, which they themselves, by mutual covenants, have fastened at one end, to the lips of that Man, or Assembly, to whom they have given the Soveraigne Power; and at the other end to their own Ears. These Bonds in their own nature but weak, may nevertheless be made to hold, by the danger, though not by the difficulty of breaking them." Hobbes, *Leviathan*, 263–264.

46. See for example, David Gauthier, *The Logic of Leviathan*, Jean Hampton, *Hobbes and the Social Contract Tradition*, Kavka, *Hobbesian Moral and Political Theory* (rule egoism), Thomas Nagel, "Hobbes's Concept of Obligation," *The Philosophical Review* 59 (1959): 68–83.

47. See for example, A. E. Taylor, "The Ethical Doctrine of Hobbes," *Philosophy*, 13 (October 1938): 406–424, Howard Warrender, *The Political Philosophy of Hobbes, His Theory of Obligation* (Oxford: Clarendon Press, 1957).

48. Hobbes, *Leviathan*, 215.

49. Hobbes, *Leviathan*, 215.

50. Hobbes, *Leviathan*, 216–217.

51. Hobbes, *Leviathan*, J. C. A. Gaskin (ed.) (New York: Oxford University Press, 1996), xxxiii.

52. Hobbes, *Leviathan*, Gaskin ed., xxxiv.

53. Hobbes, *Leviathan*, 1968, 409.

54. Hobbes, Leviathan, 409.

55. Hobbes, Leviathan, 85.

56. Hobbes, Leviathan, 1968, 223.

57. Hobbes, Leviathan, 1968, 272.

58. The reason for confining my analysis of Hobbes's theory of rights to that given in *Leviathan* is that he strengthens the theory in *Leviathan* from that of earlier versions given in the *Elements of Law* or *De Cive*.

59. Hobbes, *Leviathan*, 189.

60. Hobbes, *Leviathan*, 189.

61. Thomas Hobbes, "The Elements of Law," in *Human Nature and De Corpore Politico*, ed., J. C. A. Gaskin (Oxford: Oxford University Press, 1994), 80.

62. Thomas Hobbes, "The Elements of Law," 80.

63. It has a been a mistake of much commentary to see the liberties held under the right of nature as the exemplars of Hobbesian rights instead of as the starting point from which Hobbes develops his argument regarding which rights should exist within civil society, which must be given up and which should be protected.

64. Simmons, *The Lockean Theory of Rights*, 92.

65. Simmons, *The Lockean Theory of Rights*.

66. Simmons, *The Lockean Theory of Rights*.

67. Simmons, *The Lockean Theory of Rights*, 93.

68. Locke, *Second Treatise*, 111.

69. Dunn, *The Political Thought of John Locke*, 267.

Chapter 4

The Jurisprudential Turn
in Rights Theorising

RIGHTS IN LAW

Having speculated in the last chapter about whether Hobbes's theory of rights would have been a more appropriate candidate for providing a forerunner for modern rights theory than Locke's, I shall now return to the reality of how the history of rights theory developed, with the jurisprudential turn in rights theorising. As theories of natural law and natural rights were increasingly seen to be unsustainable against the criticisms of the empiricists and positivists, the notion of individual rights was in need of a new justification and explanation. The question that needed to be answered was, in what sense can individual rights be said to exist if they do not exist as dictates of a natural law (and usually) stamped with the unassailable moral authority of God's plan for mankind? Where else might rights come from if not from the universal morality of natural law?

The loss of a natural law justification for rights within mainstream jurisprudence and political philosophy, leaves a large theoretical hole to fill, and one could say that philosophers and jurists have been trying to fill that hole ever since. The dominant influence on rights theory since the demise of natural law has come from analytical jurisprudence. This is hardly surprising. As natural law lost its dominance within philosophy of law, it was replaced with the new positivism. And, as positivism stripped morality out of law, we were left with a view of law as empirical fact; verifiable and solid and without any need to appeal to metaphysics or theology. If we want to find where rights exist in a factual sense, we need look no further than actual positive law, where the rights of particular individuals, correlated with the duties of others, have not only always been visible but also have teeth. When those with legal duties towards legal right holders fail to perform those duties there is legal redress. Legal rights are enforceable in a way that purely moral rights cannot be. It is worth noting though, that as the philosophical examination of rights moved away from the province of natural law and into that of analytical jurisprudence it meant that the philosophy of rights moved away from a focus on moral and political principles, in seeking explanations and justifications for rights and instead looked more to conceptual analysis and the role and function of legal rights, in order to seek an understanding of what rights are.

We can start our examination of the next stage in the history of rights theory at the exact point we left off the last stage, with the discrediting of natural rights. When natural rights sustained their greatest attack from Bentham, he also gave us, at the same time, the answer to the question that would result from his attack. If there are no natural rights, what kind of rights are there, if any? In one of his remarks attacking natural rights, quoted in the last chapter, he tells us "right is with me the child of law: . . . A natural right is a son that never had a father."[1] With these metaphors we could say that he ushers in the era of the jurisprudence of rights. The task of explaining and justifying rights will be taken up by those working in philosophy of law and the influence of the work done on the jurisprudence of rights, particularly in the early twentieth century, still dominates rights theory today. The most influential of the writers within jurisprudence, apart from Bentham himself, is, arguably, Wesley Hohfeld. Hohfeld's analysis of the term "right" and how it is used in the legal literature is widely acknowledged as a brilliant piece of analytical jurisprudence and has been used as the template for many rights theorists in moral and political philosophy as well as in jurisprudence, up to the present time. His influence is such that his notion of the "claim right" has come to be seen as the exemplar of a moral and political right as well as a legal right. As Jeremy Waldron puts it, "Hohfeld's *claim-right* is generally regarded as coming closest to capturing the concept of individual rights used in political morality."[2]

HOHFELD'S ANALYSIS OF RIGHTS

American jurist Wesley Hohfeld died young but left, in the form of articles and essays (that were posthumously published as a book), an analysis of rights in law.[3] The definitions he provides in that analysis have become accepted to the point that they are now used, often without any discussion or justification, by most of those working on the subject of rights within jurisprudence and political philosophy. The influence of the Hohfeldian analysis is ubiquitous. It is worth mentioning that in the view of H. L. A. Hart, Jeremy Bentham "anticipated much of Hohfeld's work" and is "a more thought-provoking guide than Hohfeld."[4] However, he also acknowledges that Bentham's "doctrine has to be collected from observations scattered through his voluminous and not always very readable works."[5] And more importantly, at least for my purposes, it is Hohfeld's analysis that has been the influential one and so it is to Hohfeld that we should turn in this next stage of the history of rights theory.

Hohfeld's Categories of Rights

Hohfeld picks out four different senses in which the term "right" is used in law to describe specific legal relations between at least two people. According to Hohfeld, all uses of the term "right" in the legal literature can be captured by using one of the four categories of right that he picks out. Each category or "incident" of right also has a legal correlative and a legal opposite, as they each define a legal relationship between two or more persons (see below, tables 4.1 and 4.2). The four categories or incidents are: claim, privilege (liberty), power, and immunity.

Claim

A claim right exists when I have a right to X such that at least one other person Y, has a duty to me, to allow me to have or to do X, or to give me X, or refrain from X. So, for example, I have a claim right not to be assaulted and this means that all others have a duty not to assault me. I have a claim right to exclusive use of this laptop, which means that all others have a duty not to use this laptop (unless I give them permission to use it).

Privilege (Liberty)

The Hohfeldian privilege, often referred to as a "liberty right," exists when I have a right to X such that I have no duty not to X or not to have X and no one else has a claim right with the correlative duty that I should not X or have X. For example, if I have a liberty right to the apples on the tree then I have no duty not to take the apples on the tree and no one else has a claim right to the apples on the tree. (If someone did have a claim right to the apples then it would mean that I would have a duty not to take the apples.)

So, if all the people in the orchard have liberty rights to the apples on the tree, then each and every one of them has a right to try to take the apples and no one has a duty to stand out of their way. In other words, everyone is free to take the apples. We might say there is a free-for-all to see who will get the apples. We could all run up to the tree and try to pick the apples. This is why liberty rights are sometimes said to be "competitive rights." All the people in the orchard will be potentially competing against each other to try and get the apples. Liberty rights are also said to be "bare freedoms." This is a response to the fact that liberty rights have no "built in" protections—they are not directly correlated with duties in the way that claim rights are. I will say much more about this later, in my critique of the way in which the Hohfeldian analysis has been used in rights theory. For now, it is enough to see that his category of privilege or liberty right is characterized by the lack of directly correlated duties to protect the right.

Power

A power is a right to alter the legal rights and duties of others. The example often given is of my right to make a will. When I make my will, I have the legal power to alter the rights and duties of certain other people. If I make X executor, then I have given X legal duties which she did not have before. My power right in relation to X whom I make executor, is correlated with a legal liability on the part of X, because X is liable to having her legal situation changed by me when I exercise my right to make a will. If I then make Y a beneficiary of my will, Y's legal situation is changed because Y now has legal rights, to inherit from me, that he did not have before.

Immunity

I have an immunity when I am protected from the liability of having my legal situation changed. When I have an immunity right to X then at least one other person has no power or has a disability in relation to me. In other words that other person, Y, is unable to take away my right to X. An example often used is the American Bill of Rights which consists of a list of immunities held by American citizens. The right to free speech is one such right. It cannot be limited or taken away even by the legislature.

It can be helpful to see these legal correlatives and opposites (contradictories) in table form:

Table 4.1   Legal Opposites

If A has a claim	then A lacks a no-claim
If A has a privilege (liberty)	then A lacks a duty
If A has a power	then A lacks a disability
If A has an immunity	then A lacks a liability

Table 4.2   Legal Correlatives

If A has a claim	then some other person B has a duty
If A has a privilege (liberty)	then some other person B has a no-claim
If A has a power	then some other person B has a liability
If A has an immunity	then some other person B has a disability

Table 4.3   Legal correlatives and opposites (contradictories)

Right	Liberty	Power	Immunity
Duty	No-right	Liability	Disability

Each column shows a pair of legal correlatives, each diagonal, a pair of legal opposites.

The Significance of the Claim Right

Of the four categories of right it is the claim right that has been picked out, by jurists and political philosophers (and also by Hohfeld himself), as being the category of right that most accurately captures what we mean by a right. My right to free speech, for example, is correlated with the duties of others (and the state) to allow me to speak freely (with the usual sorts of provisos about it not clashing with other more important rights/duties which may override it such as the duty not to incite violence). Though it is worth noting that if I was a U.S. citizen my right to free speech would also be an immunity.

Hohfeld himself picked out the claim right as the only right which is, in his terminology, properly called a right. He says, "A duty is the invariable correlative of that legal relation which is most properly called a right or claim."[6] It was nothing new to point out the importance of the relationship of rights to duties. Moral philosophers have often argued that rights are no more than the "other side" of duties, leading some to conclude that the concept of a right has no independent existence and that all we really need to talk about are duties.[7] They argue, in other words, that the significant moral concept is *duty* rather than *right*. What the Hohfeldian analysis did that was new, was to make the correlation between a right and a duty definitional (see table 4.2). This meant that it was no longer a relationship open to discussion but rather an indisputable connection. If there is a right, then there is a duty on the part of at least one other. I will discuss the implications of this in much greater detail in chapter 6.

COMPLEX RIGHTS

Rights that we hold are often complex rights, Hohfeld tells us, that combine together two or more of his "incidents." So, for example, property rights are typically complex rights that consist of a cluster of simple or "atomic" rights. My right to my house consists of a claim right, which is correlated with the duty of all other people who do not own the house, to refrain from anything that would interfere with my ownership rights including entering the house without my permission. It also consists of my liberty right to walk around my house, which is correlated with the "no-right" of all non-owners who, in other words have no claim that I should not, that is, they cannot tell me I have a duty not to (see table 4.2). I have a power right to leave the house to a person of my choosing and thus alter their legal position in relation to the house. I also have a power right to waive my claim to sole occupation of the house and allow others to also occupy it. None of these rights is absolute; they can be altered by, for example, the state having a right to take my property during a time of war. My right to do things in my house does not extend to a right to manufacture or grow illegal drugs in it.

The Significance of Hohfeld's Analysis

Hohfeld's analysis is significant in several ways which will be explored in more detail in chapter 6, where I offer a critique of the way in which the Hofeldian system is used in recent and current rights theory. First, Hohfeld's analysis picks out the *claim* as the exemplar of what it is to be a right. Second, it separates the notion of *liberty* from the notion of a *right*. In historical discussions of natural rights, the words "right" and "liberty" are often used interchangeably.[8] Third, it sees the relationship between a right and a duty (on the part of another to uphold, protect, provide etc. that right), as a relationship of logic or analysis or definition. This relationship of strict correlativity leaves no room for other, more loosely connected duties that might also be effective to uphold, protect etc. the right in question.

It is important to point out that Hohfeld never claimed that his analysis amounted to a *theory* of rights. He was attempting, rather, to provide a comprehensive analysis of the term "right" as it is used in the legal literature. He did not set out to provide a full *theory* of rights, so he makes no attempt to justify or explain the existence of rights. Nor does he try to justify the system of rights he describes as part of a broader moral or political theory. This makes the Hohfeldian *analysis of legal rights* quite distinct from *theories of natural rights* and, for that matter, from other modern theories of rights.

Although Hohfeld does not venture into moral theory, it is worth noting that his understanding of rights is stripped of all reference to the moral philosophy (often as attached to Christian theology), that is found in theories of natural rights. Hohfeld's analysis of rights, while not a *theory* of rights as such, nevertheless, takes a view of rights that, as well as being jurisprudential, is also wholly secular and, one might say, non-moral, except perhaps in the use of the moral term "duty." If one takes the term "duty" in his analysis to refer to purely legal duties, however, then it leaves open the question of whether any, some, or all, of the duties he describes, are moral duties in addition to being legal duties.

Hohfeld, then, fixes on the *claim* as the concept which defines what a right is. And he also proposes that rights are relational; they define a relationship between at least two legal persons (see tables 4.1, 4.2 and 4.3). His work leaves us with a sharp analysis of the legal concept of a right as it is already used in law. It refrains from developing a theory of rights that might explain or justify the notion of rights that individuals may hold and it also refrains from introducing any moral or political principles that might inform such a theory. But the analytical jurisprudential era in rights theory is not devoid of attempts to create a theory of rights and it is to those theories that I now turn.

Theories of Rights

In the *post natural law era* of exploring the notion of rights, there are two dominant *theories* of rights as well as the influential *analysis* of rights given by Hohfeld. And so, while Hohfeld's analysis may dominate rights theory in the sense of providing definitions of (legal) rights and their correlatives and opposites, that are used and applied in many theoretical discussions of rights; it is to the "interest" (or "benefit") and "will" (or "choice") theories of rights that we must turn for genuine *theories* of rights. M. D. A. Freeman puts it in the following way, "[t]here are two competing theories as to the nature of rights: one emphasizes will or choice; the other interest or benefit."[9] And Brian Bix makes the same point. "In the analytical tradition, there are two primary conceptual theories about the nature of rights."[10]

The "Will" or "Choice" Theory of Rights

The analytical approach of Hohfeld continues in the work of the twentieth century jurists who take up the task of explaining and justifying rights. Of the two main competing theories, it is the will theory that sees rights as emphasising the power and control of the right holder. In the words of H. L. A. Hart, one of the theory's best-known proponents, the right makes the right holder "a small-scale sovereign."[11] Crucially, the right holder has control over the duty that is correlative to her right. This means, in effect, that the right holder can choose either to hold the bearer of the duty to performance of his duty or she can waive the duty. So, for example, if I lend you £100 and you promise to pay me back, I then have a right to be paid back the £100 by you and you have a duty to pay me back the £100 but I can choose to waive the duty and tell you that it is ok, you do not have pay me back the money. The choice is mine not yours and so the right gives me control over your duty. This makes clear Hart's idea that the right makes one "a small-scale sovereign" with power and control over the duty of whoever has the duty that is correlative to the right.

The full quote from Hart is,

> [t]he idea is that of one individual being given by the law exclusive control, more or less extensive, over another person's duty so that in the area of conduct

covered by that duty, the individual who has the right is a small-scale sovereign to whom the duty is owed. The fullest measure of control comprises three distinguishable elements: (i) the right holder may waive or extinguish the duty or leave it in existence; (ii) after breach or threatened breach of a duty he may leave it "unenforced" or may "enforce" it suing for compensation or, in certain cases, for an injunction or mandatory order to restrain the continued or further breach of duty; and (iii) he may waive or extinguish the obligation to pay compensation to which the breach gives rise.[12]

One of the things made absolutely clear in this passage is that Hart is discussing rights within the law. And yet, as with Hohfeld's analysis, this theory is often taken up and used by those working in moral and political philosophy on rights as well as those working within jurisprudence. On examination, it is clear that even within the law this theory does not cover all legal rights and it certainly doesn't cover all moral and political rights. As Waldron points out, Hart was aware of this. "Hart has conceded, however, that this analysis does not offer an adequate account of all legal rights, let alone the rights recognized in social and political morality."[13] Indeed, for his chapter in Waldron's collection, Hart defends the notion of a moral right in his proposal that "if there are any moral rights at all, it follows that there is at least one natural right, the equal right of all men to be free."[14] The right he proposes is subject to waivers and provisos to the point that it is scarcely a natural right in the traditional sense, as he himself points out, but it is never-the-less an admission that there can be *moral rights* as well as *legal rights*. It is also of interest that he is prepared to say that there is, at least in this case, what we might call a *natural right,* though it seems likely that by this he simply means a universal, moral right.

It is also clear that, unlike Hohfeld, Hart introduces a political concept when he talks of a right holder as a "small scale sovereign." This idea of the right holder as sovereign empowers her and gives her the autonomy and freedom to make choices that affect her. One could say that this way of explaining a right is therefore providing a justification of rights in terms of such values as individual autonomy and liberty. One could also say that a right, according to this theory, is a kind of power, in as much as the right holder has the power to affect the duties of the duty holder(s).

A common objection that has been made to the "will" or "choice" theory of rights, historically, is that there are important rights that cannot be accommodated within its definitions. So, for example, children cannot be said to have rights as they do not have the capacity to make the appropriate choices or have the appropriate powers over the correlative duty. Similarly, there cannot be rights for unconscious patients or those without capacity for other reasons. Another common objection is that there can be no inalienable rights under the choice theory because the theory cannot allow for situations in which the duty cannot be waived by the right holder. Yet, most people believe that some rights should be or are inalienable (Neil MacCormick has been critical of Hart's will theory on this point).[15] For example, if my right to life is correlated with your duty not to kill me then I should not be able to waive your duty not to kill me.

The "Interest" or "Benefit" Theory of Rights

The interest or benefit theory, in contrast to the choice theory, emphasizes what the right holder *gains* by having the right. It is said that holding the right protects or furthers the interests of the right holder or brings her a benefit. In other words, for the interest theorist, the most important characteristic of a right is that it represents something of benefit to the right holder, something which it is in their interests to have.

The original "benefit" theorist is Jeremy Bentham and in his thorough and detailed discussion of Bentham's analysis of rights, Hart points out that Bentham is providing an analysis of rights in law that seeks to "fix" definitions of terms (as used in law). Hart refers to this methodology as "rational reconstruction" or "refinement of concepts in use."[16] He then notes that Bentham picks out three of what will later be the Hohfeldian incidents— claim, liberty, and power. But what concerns us here is his interest theory of rights, rather than his entire analysis of rights. Bentham claims that a person has a right if someone else has a duty to perform an act or omission which is in the right holder's interest. "[W]ith the exception of 'barren' and 'self-regarding' obligation *all* obligations, civil or criminal, have correlative rights held by those intended to benefit by their performance."[17] This applies to classes of people as well as to individuals. We must know in advance whose interests the duty will further. It is clear from this very short summary that for Bentham at least, there is strict correlativity between rights and duties. The correlativity is so strict that one may follow either a right to find the duty or a duty to find the right. In other words, whenever there is a duty there is a correlative right and vice versa.

This is not the case in all versions of the interest theory. Neil MacCormick, for example, argues against the notion that rights are strictly, or by definition, correlated with duties.[18] Instead, he argues that rights are *reasons for imposing* a duty or for providing some other form of protection of the interests of the rights holder. The difference is significant and marks MacCormick out as anti-Hohfeldian. By saying that a right is a reason for imposing a duty, MacCormick is saying that rights have their own status, their own independent existence, separate from any corresponding duties. When you have strict correlativity between rights and duties, on the other hand, then the right can be said to be nothing more than the "other side" of the duty; to have no independence as a concept beyond what is implied by a duty or a legal obligation.

Another way of talking about rights under this theory also stresses the lack of focus, one might almost say, on the right itself. In order to qualify as a right, according to the interest theory, one must be able to say to whose benefit the performance of the duty is, in advance. To return to the example of promising to repay a loan of one hundred pounds. If I am repaid the money, many people might benefit, including, for example, my friend when I buy her lunch. But my friend has no right to that benefit, to be paid any money. As Waldron puts it, "[a] benefit giving rise to a right must be so intimately related to the duty that it is possible to say in advance that unless this benefit is conferred, the duty has not been carried out."[19] So, in the case of the promise, it is only the benefit to you of receiving the money from me when I perform my duty that gives rise to a right attached to you, to receive the money from me.

MacCormick, in his version of interest theory, argues that there are three features "which must be included in any characterization of rules which confer rights."[20] The first is that "they concern "goods" (or "advantages" or "benefits" or "interests" or however we may express the point). Whatever X may be, the idea of anyone's having a right to X would be absurd unless it were presupposed that X is normally a good for human beings, at any rate for those people who qualify for the right in question."[21] The second feature of rights is that "they concern the enjoyment of goods by individuals separately,"[22] rather than communally. The third feature is that "benefits are secured to individuals in that the law provides normative protection for individuals in their enjoyment of them."[23]

Joseph Raz's version of the interest theory also sees a right as *a reason for imposing* a duty rather than automatically correlated with a duty. On Raz's account, "X has a right if X can have rights, and, other things being equal, an aspect of X's well-being (his interest) is a sufficient reason for holding some other person(s) to be under a duty."[24]

Established Criticism of the Will and Interest Theories

Much ink has been spilled in criticising these two theories. Certain criticisms established themselves over time, the most important being perhaps, the one that applies to both theories; that they are both subject to counterexamples; instances of rights (or what are commonly regarded as rights), that do not fall within one or other of the explanations of what a right is. In other words, neither of these theories succeeds in providing a completely satisfactory account of what a right is. So, for the will theory we have the counterexamples: children's rights, the rights of unconscious patients, the rights of people with dementia or other mental incapacity and generally, inalienable or nonwaivable rights. For the interest theory we have various rights that it is not in my interests to hold such as the right to be executor of your will. Also benefits to third parties where the intended beneficiary of a duty is not always seen as the holder of the correlative right. One could argue that there are more significant counterexamples to the will theory than to the interest theory. Indeed, the benefit theory is strongly intuitive. We are inclined to think of rights as in some sense representing our interests and that when our rights are protected that will be to our benefit.

There are also criticisms of the theory in question beyond the general point that they allow for counterexamples. MacCormick criticizes the will theory for failing "to include as rights some of the most important rights we have," and he gives the example of the right not to be seriously assaulted. The will theory cannot allow such a right, he says, because "no valid consent can be given which releases the assaulting party from the duty of non-interference."[25] He goes on, "[i]t is rather bewildering to suppose that none of us has a right not to be this grievously assaulted, simply because for various reasons of policy the law denies us the power to consent to these graver interferences with our physical security."[26]

Another way of putting this criticism would be to say that the will theory cannot include any inalienable or unwaivable rights and MacCormick does say this in the context of his comments on children's rights. The will theory has a problem when it comes to children's rights and he puts this problem in stark terms.

> Either we abstain from ascribing to children a right to care and nurture [on the ground that no one has discretion to waive the responsible adult's duty of care and nurture] or we abandon the will theory. For my part I have no inhibitions about abandoning the latter. It causes me no conceptual shock or mental cramp to say that children have that right. What is more, I will aver that it is *because* children have that right that it is good that legal provision should be made in the first instance to encourage and assist parents to fulfil their duty of care and nurture, and secondarily to provide for its performance by alternative foster parents when natural parents are disqualified by death, incapacity or wilful and persistent neglect.[27]

Not only does the will theory have a problem with inalienable rights but "if the will theory is correct, the more they are inalienable, the less they are rights."[28]

The debate between the two theories continues into the present day and I shall say something about more contemporary versions of that debate in chapter 7. For now, it is sufficient to note that both theories attempt to locate the primary characteristics of a right and in so doing each one characterizes a right according to certain features that are deemed to be necessary in order for something to qualify as a right. As can be seen above, neither succeeds, in the sense that they both leave out some (of what are generally agreed to be) rights. One recent solution has been to try to form a "hybrid" theory and that will be discussed in chapter 7.

Changes in the Philosophy of Rights

If we were to compare the modern jurisprudential era of rights theorizing to that of the natural law era, we could pick out several significant differences. First, of course, the move away from arguing from theological and metaphysical premises; second, the move away from an emphasis on moral and political principles (as well as jurisprudence) to an approach that is primarily jurisprudential; and third, a change in methodology. The post natural law era work on rights has marked a move to conceptual analysis and analysis of the function of rights and how they operate in the law. Leif Wenar, for example, in his entry on rights in the *Stanford Encyclopedia of Philosophy*, characterizes the will and interest theories as theories of the "function of rights." "Each theory presents itself as capturing an ordinary understanding of what rights do for those who hold them."[29] So, as well as analysis of the function of rights we also have a reference to a focus on ordinary language, to examine how the term "right" is used, in order to better understand what rights are.

NOTES

1. Jeremy Bentham, "Supply without Burthern" (1793) (London: J. Debrett, 1795).

2. Jeremy Waldron ed., *Theories of Rights* (Oxford: Oxford University Press, 1984), 8.

3. Wesley Hohfeld, *Fundamental Legal Conceptions: As Applied in Judicial Reasoning* (New Haven: Yale University Press, 1919).

4. H. L. A. Hart, *Essays on Bentham: Jurisprudence and Political Theory* (Oxford: Oxford University Press, 1982), 162.

5. Hart, *Essays on Bentham*, 162.

6. Hohfeld, *Fundamental Legal Conceptions*, 39.

7. O'Neill is an example of a moral philosopher who is sceptical about the notion of rights detached from specific duties. As she has puts it, "without obligation there are no rights." Onora O'Neill, "The Dark Side of Human Rights," *International Affairs*, 81, no. 2 (2005): 431.

8. "The Freedom men were under apart from that law was now described in terms of their natural rights." Richard Tuck, *Natural Rights Theories: Their Origin and Development* (Cambridge: Cambridge University Press, 1979).

9. M. D. A. Freeman, *Lloyd's Introduction to Jurisprudence*, 8th ed. (London: Sweet and Maxwell, 2008), 394.

10. Brian Bix, *Jurisprudence: Theory and Context* (London: Sweet and Maxwell, 2006), 129.

11. H. L. A. Hart, *Essays on Bentham*, 183.

12. Hart, *Essays on Bentham*, 183–184.

13. Waldron ed., *Theories of Rights*, 9.

14. H. L. A. Hart, "Are There Any Natural Rights," in *Theories of Rights*, ed. Jeremy Waldron (Oxford: Oxford University Press: 1984), 77.

15. D. N. MacCormick, "Rights in Legislation," in *Law, Morality and Society: Essays in Honour of H. L. A. Hart*, eds. P. Hacker and J. Raz (Oxford: Oxford University Press, 1977), 198–199.

16. H. L. A. Hart, *Essays on Bentham*, 164.

17. H. L. A. Hart, *Essays on Bentham*, 174.

18. MacCormick, "Rights in Legislation," 200–201.

19. Waldron ed., *Theories of Rights*, 10.

20. MacCormick, "Rights in Legislation," 204.

21. MacCormick, "Rights in Legislation," 204.

22. MacCormick, "Rights in Legislation," 205.

23. MacCormick, "Rights in Legislation," 205.

24. Joseph Raz, *The Morality of Freedom* (Oxford: Oxford University Press, 1986), 166.

25. MacCormick, "Rights in Legislation," 197.

26. MacCormick, "Rights in Legislation," 197

27. MacCormick, "Rights in Legislation," 198.

28. MacCormick, "Rights in Legislation," 199.

29. Leif Wenar, "Rights," in *The Stanford Encyclopedia of Philosophy* (2005; last modified 2020), https://plato.stanford.edu/archives/spr2021/entries/rights/. "There are two main theories of the function of rights: the will theory and the interest theory. Each theory presents itself as capturing an ordinary understanding of what rights do for those who hold them. Which theory offers the better account of the function of rights has been the subject of spirited dispute, literally for ages."

Chapter 5

Reading Historical Writing on Rights

The Distorting Influence of Hohfeld

One illustration of the ubiquity of the influence of the Hohfeldian analysis on modern rights theorising, is its use by those writing on historical rights theories. The following passage from A. John Simmons on Locke's theory of rights makes the point.

> Locke never gives us anything like a definition of a right in his works. . . . But careful attention to the ways in which Locke uses the concept of right in his arguments allows some safe assumptions about his position. We can distinguish (although Locke himself does not) four kinds of rights at work in the *Treatises*. There is first (and least important) what is commonly referred to as a "liberty" or "liberty right" (following Hohfeld). This is a right only in the limited sense that one has a "right" to do what is morally permissible to do (what is "alright"); a liberty right is the mere absence of an obligation to refrain. Such rights are not protected by correlative duties on the part of others to respect or allow performance of the right, and hence are "competitive" with the liberty rights of others. Liberty rights exist where "the law of nature is silent."[1]

Simmons then goes on to speculate when Locke must "have in mind" liberty rights and proposes that the right to "appropriate by our labour some particular unowned good"[2] would be just such a right. He claims that Locke "never intends to argue that others are bound to *allow* me to appropriate any particular good, that they may not labour on and appropriate it first. The duties of others are only to obey the law of nature in attempts to appropriate (by, e.g., not using violence, leaving enough and as good for others) and to respect others' property once it has been established by labour."[3]

First, it is always unwise to state what a historical figure intended without any clear evidence of such intentions. I would argue that we cannot know that

Locke "never intends to argue" something. We can only speculate in the light of the evidence we have of what he does argue. I would suggest that Simmons is trying to fit Locke's theory of natural rights into the Hohfeldian analysis. When he says in the passage above that Locke himself does not use the four Hohfeldian categories of rights, he adds in a footnote that "Locke's use of various synonyms for right—power, title, privilege, claim, liberty—does not, unfortunately, signal any substantive distinctions, as far as I can tell."[4] So, on the one hand he is arguing that Locke does not seem to differentiate between these different terms and on the other he argues that Locke "had in mind" Hohfeldian liberty rights when he discusses the appropriation of property through labour.

The next footnote is also worth looking at. Simmons says the following,

> Because of the legal origin of rights-talk, Hohfeld's analysis is an appropriate place to start talking about *moral* rights, despite the fact that Hohfeld discusses only the various types of *legal* rights (or "senses" the word "right" has in the law). . . . The four legal relations Hohfeld distinguishes—liberty (or privilege), (claim) right (or right in the "strict sense"), power, and immunity—are usefully employed in classifying *moral* relations as well. I think we can clearly find the first three in the *Treatises* as types of *moral* rights, while Locke's insistence on the imprescriptibility of natural rights might be taken to signal a moral immunity (of a sort). The basic distinction between liberties and claim rights, of course, was at work in many natural rights theories before Locke, but the first really precise formulation came rather later, in Bentham.[5]

The first sentence is particularly puzzling. Presumably, when Simmons refers to "the legal origin of rights-talk," he is referring to the fact that legal relations between individuals have always involved legal duties or obligations and their correlative legal rights, or legal rights and their correlative legal duties. So, my right to occupy the house I have legal title to implies your duty to stay out of my house unless invited in. The sentence gets more puzzling when Simmons adds, "Hohfeld's analysis is an appropriate place to start talking about *moral* rights, despite the fact that Hohfeld discusses only the various types of *legal* rights (or "senses" the word "right" has in the law)." Why is Hohfeld's analysis an appropriate place to start talking about moral rights? Why in particular is it the right place to start talking about moral rights when, a) Hohfeld states that he is only analysing the use of the legal term "right" and b) Locke's theory of rights (as the theory under discussion) is explicitly concerned with the moral theory of *natural rights*, attached to *natural law*? Simmons doesn't tell us, except to say that the four legal relations Hohfeld distinguishes "are usefully employed in classifying moral relations as well." Again, why? I will discuss this question, of the suitability of applying the Hohfeldian analysis of legal rights to an analysis of moral and political rights, in more detail in chapter 6. For now, it is important to note that this is frequently done by commentators analysing historical rights theories, and often, as with Simmons, without any argument or discussion of reasons as to why this practice might be justified.

The final sentence above is also worth drawing attention to. Simmons tells us that the "basic distinction between liberties and claim rights, of course, was at work in many natural rights theories before Locke, but the first really precise formulation came rather later, in Bentham." First, it seems odd to say that the distinction between liberties and claim rights was "at work" in many natural rights theories when theories of natural rights often refer to liberties as rights and vice versa. In other words, the terms "rights" and "liberties" are often used interchangeably, as they are, for example, in Hobbes. Or they are put side by side implying either that they are the same or very closely related.[6] Natural rights are also often said to refer to a power or faculty. Tuck writing on Jean Gerson argues that "for the Romans and early medieval law-yers liberty could not be 'a ius, a right.'" But Gerson, "by claiming that ius was a facultas . . . was able to assimilate ius and libertas."[7] Gerson says "*Ius* is a *facultas* or power appropriate to someone and in accordance with the dictates of right reason. *Libertas* is a *facultas* of the reason and will towards whatever possibility is selected."[8] Another way the relationship between right and liberty is sometimes conceived is that there is a right to liberty. So, for example, Tierney points out that Las Casas, writing about the natural rights of the Native American Indians under Spanish rule, argues that the Indians had "a right to liberty, a right to own property, a right of self-defence, a right to form their own governments."[9]

Clearly, these sorts of rights depend upon the actions or inactions and the duties of others. And so, we might say, they are Hofeldian claim rights. And yet, one of these "claim rights" is a so-called liberty. This illustrates the difficulty of trying to interpret historical theories of natural rights using the Hohfeldian analysis. There are complicated and subtle matters of political morality under discussion and the concept of *natural rights* is, at this time, fluid and constantly changing in relation to other concepts. I argue that the complex relationship between the use of the terms, "liberty" and "right" within historical discussions of *natural rights*, cannot always be captured by the Hohfeldian definitions.

It is also the case that while we can find instances where the term "right" is used to describe a claim to the duties of others (e.g. in Grotius), there are also instances where *liberties* describe claims to the duties of others in this way (e.g. in Hobbes). And Simmons says, as above, that Locke also uses the terms *right* and *liberty* (in addition to others) interchangeably. It could be argued that historical writers are "really describing Hohfeldian incidents/categories of right," even though the language and terminology they use is sometimes confusing or indeed confused. This is the sort of argument made or rather assumed by Simmons and many other commentators. The argument assumes that Hohfeld has it right with his categories and historical writers sometimes get it right and sometimes get it wrong or sometimes have to be reinterpreted until we can see how they are in fact describing Hohfeldian categories of rights even if it does not seem as though they are (as in Simmons above).

One problem with this sort of argument is that it means that we must either fit the historical discussions of rights into the Hohfeldian categories where we can, as Simmons does with Locke, or, where we can't, presumably we should reject outright the discussion. This seems unsatisfactory. The language of rights, as I say, is fluid in historical discussions. Writers are feeling their way with the new idea that all individuals have subjective rights that attach to them by virtue of their humanity rather than being attached to a particular role or legal status. A useful example to illustrate this comes from Grotius who (as discussed in chapter 1), uses many definitions of what a right is or can be and describes many different kinds of right, some of which hark back to the old objective use of right as analogous to justice or what is objectively right according to natural law and some of which try to capture the new subjective notion of natural rights.

> There is another signification of the word RIGHT, . . . which relates directly to the person. In which sense, RIGHT is a moral quality annexed to the person, justly entitling him to possess some particular privilege, or to perform some particular act.
>
> . . . Right, strictly taken, is again twofold, the one, PRIVATE, established for the advantage of each individual, the other SUPERIOR, as involving the claims, which the state has upon individuals, and their property, for the public good. . . . There is also a third signification of the word Right, which has the same meaning as Law, taken in its most extensive sense, to denote a rule of moral action, obliging us to do what is proper.[10]

It is clear from these passages that Grotius is using the term "right" to describe several different kinds of right or as he puts it, different "significations" of the word "right." The first describes a subjective right as a just entitlement to something or to do something. He also says it describes a moral quality, so he is describing a kind of moral right. In the next passage, Grotius makes a distinction between rights which are "private" and to the advantage of each individual and the rights of the state over their citizens. The former, again sounding very much like other descriptions of subjective "natural" rights, while the latter, in contrast, describing the political/legal rights of states in relations to their citizens. The last section defines natural right as natural law. This refers back to the older understanding of natural right as the same as natural law, setting out what is forbidden according to natural law, as dictated by reason and commanded by God.

If we insist on analysing such passages using only the Hofeldian catego-ries, we risk losing elements of our historical understanding of how the notion of natural rights evolves and develops. And, of course, we also lose entirely those parts of the description of rights that refer purely to moral rights and particularly to rights as connected to parts of Christian theology and the moral philosophy that comes from it. This means leaving out important moral con-cepts that are entwined within the theory of natural rights such as the notion of *natural equality*, coming from the belief of the late medieval and early modern Christian writers, that all humans are created as equals by God. It is this notion of *natural equality* that underlies the notion of universal natural rights, held equally by all human beings, simply by virtue of their humanity. And we only have to look to Locke to see a clear example of the use of this reasoning to arrive at a theory of natural rights.

The *state of nature* has a law of nature to govern it, which obliges every one: and reason, which is that law, teaches all mankind, who will but consult it, that being *all equal and independent,* no one ought to harm another in his life, health, liberty, or possessions. And that all men be restrained from invad-ing others rights.[11]

One question raised by the use of the Hohfeldian categories to analyse his-torical writers on natural rights is whether this can prevent a full examination of the moral and political elements of the theories. If the entire analysis of the notion of individual rights is, as it were, accomplished by the Hohfeldian analysis, then there is no conceptual space for moral/political content within the notion of a right.

Another significant drawback to analysing historical writers on rights using only the Hohfeldian analysis is that it can lead to distorted "readings" of his-torical texts. One such distorted reading has become common within Hobbes scholarship. Scholarship on Locke, as mentioned above, is also affected by such distorted readings. The rest of this chapter will be given over to a detailed exposition of the distorted reading of Hobbes's theory of rights that has resulted from this approach.

THE HOHFELDIAN READING OF HOBBES'S THEORY OF RIGHTS

It is an orthodoxy of Hobbes scholarship over the last seventy years or so that Hobbes's theory of rights is weak and inconsequential. According to this view, individual subjects in a Hobbesian commonwealth do not hold any significant rights and certainly none that would offer a defence for subjects against an all-powerful sovereign. The arguments that are marshalled to support this are almost always constructed using a Hohfeldian analysis of rights. Hobbes's descriptions of the rights of subjects are interpreted using Hohfeldian terminology and applying his categories of rights, particularly those of "privilege" (liberty) and "claim" (right).

Simply put, it is argued that all the subjects' rights described in Hobbes's political theory are Hohfeldian *liberty rights* (or "privileges"). This means that, by definition, there are no correlative duties on the part of others to respect or protect such rights; hence the argument that these are weak, ineffectual rights that offer no protections to subjects. According to this reading of the theory, none of the subjects' rights described by Hobbes are Hohfeldian *claim rights*. None, in other words, are rights "in the strictest sense"[12] (according to Hohfeld). So, the argument is that Hobbes's theory of rights isn't a genuine theory of individual rights at all but merely an account of natural liberties or "bare freedoms" that offer no protections to Hobbesian subjects and no check on the power of the sovereign.

Commentators on Hobbes have frequently drawn the conclusion that Hobbes's theory of rights is weak from the argument that the Hohfeldian liberty right or "privilege" accurately describes a Hobbesian right.[13] Taking all subjects' rights to be liberty rights, they conclude that these rights are never correlated with the duties of others, that Hobbesian subjects can hold no rights against the sovereign and therefore that there are no genuine political rights for subjects in the theory.[14]

> . . . the modern conception of what it means to have a right stands in stark contrast with Hobbes's conception of rights as "blameless liberties." The presence of a Hobbesian right has only one effect: it determines the moral status of a person's action when exercising the right. Having a Hobbesian right to some action only signifies that the action is morally permissible and that the actor has not committed an injustice. Acting with right has no normative effect on anyone else; *no one has a duty to respect the right.* . . .
>
> The feebleness of Hobbes's notion of a right stands in contrast with the current notion. Today, it is believed that if someone has a right to something, then, at least prima facie, others have a correlative duty to respect the exercise of that right.[15]

This quotation, from Susanne Sreedhar's book on "resistance" in Hobbes's political theory, illustrates nicely how the Hohfeldian analysis of rights is employed in arguments seeking to show the weakness of Hobbesian rights. In this instance, the Hohfeldian analysis is taken for granted to such an extent that it is not mentioned, even in a footnote. (Hohfeld's *Legal Conceptions* is in the bibliography however, so we need not speculate that the use of a Hohfeldian analysis is unconscious or accidental). One Hobbes scholar who does acknowledge the Hohfeldian source of her analysis is Jean Hampton. In her important 1986 book, *Hobbes and the Social Contract Tradition,*[16] she lists the four meanings or "incidents" of right that Hohfeld picks out and remarks "[t]he notion of a right as a claim is perhaps the most common and natural concept that the word "right" has been taken to cover." She then applies Hohfeld's analysis to Hobbes,

> It is easy to mistakenly assume that Hobbes uses the word "right" in this sense [as a claim right]. But he does not; in fact, his use of the word shows that he endorses the second conception of "right" outlined by Hohfeld—the idea that a right is a privilege or a liberty.[17]

Other commentators such as Gregory Kavka,[18] change the terminology slightly. He refers to liberty rights as permission rights. But the approach and analysis are still clearly Hohfeldian, as they are in Sreedhar's commentary. The conclusion is the same for all these commentators; Hobbes describes liberty rights for subjects and not claim rights. This remains a common inter-pretation of Hobbesian rights, though it has weakened a little in recent years.

As I outlined in chapter 4, The Hohfeldian liberty right, defined as a liberty or "privilege" with no correlated duties on the part of others, is a right whose legal opposite is a duty and whose legal correlative is a "no claim" or "no right."[19]

> [A] privilege is the opposite of a duty, and the correlative of a "no-right." In the example last put, [in which X owns some land] whereas X has a right or claim that Y, the other man should stay off the land, he himself has the privilege of entering on the land; or in equivalent words, X does not have a duty to stay off. The privilege of entering is the negation of a duty to stay off.[20]

So, a Hohfeldian privilege is nothing more than a lack of duty. If I have a liberty right to X then I am free to X. To be more precise, it is that liberty or privilege which is the legal correlative of the lack of a legal claim by another. No one else has a claim that I should not X. Without such a duty, I am in some sense "free" to do what I will. It is important to note how specific the Hohfeldian liberty right is. It is the legal position in which there is no legal duty not to X. Many commentators assume that the Hohfeldian analysis can be applied, without further argument or discussion to moral and political rights as well as to legal rights. For example, Mathew Kramer makes the claim that, ". . . virtually every aspect of Hohfeld's analyti-cal scheme applies as well, mutatis mutandis, to the structuring of moral relationships."[21] And Jeremy Waldron remarks, along similar lines, ". . . it is clear that Hohfeldian analytics can be used to define a logical relation between moral duty and moral right just as easily as between legal duty and legal right."[22]

I will say more about this in the next chapter, where I will argue that the Hohfeldian analysis cannot be applied in a straightforward way to moral and political rights without the loss of important components of discussions of moral and political rights. But for this discussion, it is clear that the Hohfeldian analysis is usually taken to be straightforwardly applicable to moral and political rights and specifically, in this case, to Hobbesian rights. How accurate is the assertion that all Hobbesian rights (for subjects) are Hohfeldian liberty rights? Hobbes first describes the rights that individuals have under the aggregate right of the *right of nature*.

> The RIGHT OF NATURE, which Writers commonly call *Jus Naturale*, is the Liberty each man hath, to use his own power, as he will himselfe, for the preservation of his own Nature; that is to say, of his own Life; and consequently, of doing any thing, which in his own Judgement, and Reason, hee shall conceive to be the aptest means thereunto.[23]

In a state of nature there are no laws and so the liberty he is referring to does not describe a lack of legal duty or the legal opposite of a legal duty. Hobbes infamously defines liberty as "the absence of external impediments" and I will say more about that later, but for now it is just important to note that he then *defines* a right as a liberty. "RIGHT, consisteth in liberty to do, or to forbeare;"[24] So, a right for Hobbes is a liberty, a freedom, to do something or to not do something.

In a state of nature, the liberty Hobbes describes is of the most extreme form or, to put it another way, is the most complete liberty one can imagine. It is, "a Right to every thing; even to one anothers body."[25] An individual has the right to any and all actions (or inactions) she deems necessary for her self-preservation. The right of nature comprises, as it were, a complete set of liberties; it is a state of unlimited freedom. Hobbes is quick to acknowledge that such a state of unlimited freedom is detrimental to individuals, who are unprotected in every way. " . . . [A]s long as this naturall Right of every man to every thing endureth, there can be no security to any man (how strong or wise soever he be,) of living out the time, which Nature ordinarily alloweth men to live."[26] He then describes how individuals may make life more secure by following reason and conforming to laws of nature which are rules "found out by Reason, by which a man is forbidden to do, that which is destructive of his life, or taketh away the means of preserving the same; and to omit, that, by which he thinketh it may be best preserved."[27]

Hobbes argues that (under the second law of nature) each individual must give up the right to everything and agree to only have those rights which he would be happy for all others to hold and "be contented with so much liberty against other men, as he would allow other men against himselfe."[28] He is arguing that we must give up those rights which are invasive and dangerous to others and which we therefore would not want held against ourselves, for example, the right to invade or attack the body of another. He then describes a process of the renouncing and transferring of rights across to one another and the taking on of duties "not to hinder those, to whom such right is granted, or abandoned, from the benefit of it:"[29]

> And when a man hath in either manner abandoned, or granted away his Right; then is he said to be OBLIGED, or BOUND, not to hinder those, to whom such right is granted, or abandoned, from the benefit of it: and that he *Ought,* and it is his DUTY, not to make voyd that voluntary act of his own: and that such hindrance is INJUSTICE and INJURY.[30]

Hobbes is now describing what we might call "claim rights," using Hohfeldian terminology; rights which are now correlated with duties to respect those rights. My right to your body, which I held under the right of nature, has now been given up and abandoned or transferred to you. Your right to your own body (which you already had) is now protected by my duty not to hinder you from the benefit of it.

> To *lay downe* a mans Right to any thing, is to devest himself of the *Liberty,* of hindring another of the benefit of his own Right to the same. For he that renounceth or passeth away his Right, giveth not to any other man a Right which he had not before; because there is nothing to which every man hath not Right by Nature: but onely standeth out of his way, that he may enjoy his own originall Right, without hindrance from him.[31]

Commentators on Hobbes have largely either failed to see the implications of the switch from rights as pure freedoms (under the right of nature) to rights with correlated duties (after conforming to the second law of nature), or they have argued that even though it sounds as though he is now describing claim rights he couldn't possibly be doing so for various reasons.[32] Generally, commentators argue, or assume, that all Hobbesian rights for subjects remain as liberty rights throughout the process by which he argues that individuals can move from the dangerous state of nature to life in a peaceful, orderly commonwealth. So, according to the commentators, individuals in the state of nature have a complete set of rights (liberties) while those in the Commonwealth have no rights (having given them all up to the sovereign) or a severely reduced set of rights or just the one right of self-defence, under the sovereign. While the details of interpretation differ, the main argument remains the same. Hobbes only describes Hohfeldian liberty rights for individual subjects.

One of the reasons why a Hohfeldian reading of Hobbesian rights gives such a distorted picture is that in the Hohfeldian system, actual legal rights are often complex and can be broken down into two or more categories or incidents of rights. All the incidents are fundamentally atomic and describe a legal relationship between (at least) two people.[33] This means that while rights such as property rights can comprise combinations of Hohfeldian incidents (the liberty right that I have to walk on my land, the claim right that means you must stay off my land unless invited in), there are no naturally complex incidents or categories of rights. And there is no overlap between categories or incidents of rights. Once commentators have characterised all Hobbesian subjects' rights as liberty rights (privileges) therefore, they argue that there are no claim rights for subjects in Hobbes's theory.

We can now see that there are two main reasons why Hobbesian rights have been misinterpreted when given a Hohfeldian reading. The first is that the dominance of the Hohfeldian approach to rights within political philosophy has led to the view that all political rights for individuals must have directly correlated duties on the part of others. In other words, political rights are generally defined as Hohfeldian *claim rights*. The second reason, connected to the first, is, as above, that Hobbes defines all rights as liberties and draws a distinction between liberty and obligation or duty. This is then seen by many commentators as a description of a Hohfeldian liberty right. According to the Hohfeldian analysis each Hohfeldian incident has its distinct characteristics and while different incidents can exist closely together as in the example of property rights above, there can be no movement between incidents, allowing one to change to another or to take on characteristics of another. So, when Hobbes describes the transferring and renouncing of dangerous or invasive rights that takes place when we conform to the second law of nature and the taking on of duties to respect the rights we transfer or renounce, we cannot say (using Hohfeldian terminology) that what were liberty rights have now become claim rights or that these rights are both liberties (because Hobbes defines all rights as liberties) and claims. If our analysis is to be Hohfeldian, we must stick strictly to the Hohfeldian incidents. Hence the orthodoxy that all Hobbesian rights are liberty rights and they therefore *cannot be* claim rights. And, if all political rights are claim rights (according to the dominant Hohfeldian view of rights), then there are no genuine political rights for subjects in Hobbes's theory.

I argue that there are two ways in which subjects' rights are protected in Hobbes's political theory (in *Leviathan*). The first, as already mentioned, occurs when individuals obey the second law of nature and give up those dangerous and invasive rights they held in the state of nature and take on duties not to interfere with others exercising their retained rights. The second concerns the right to self-preservation and the relationship of the subjects' rights to the duties of the sovereign.[34] Hobbes starts his political argument with the notion of self-preservation. It is our fear of death and our desire to preserve ourselves that drives us to agree to form a commonwealth. This fear and a desire, not just for life but for a good life, coupled with our reason, combine to draw us to agreement on laws of nature[35] and, on the institution of a sovereign who can enforce the laws of nature, protect the people and ensure peace and the chance of a commodious life.

Our right to preserve ourselves is our most fundamental right, according to Hobbes and while we are in the lawless *state of nature* we have a right to any action or inaction that may aid our preservation. So, we have an untrammelled freedom to preserve ourselves that has the contradictory effect of making us *less safe* as long as all others are also free to do anything, including attacking us. Once we agree to limit our right to everything, we take on duties (under the second law of nature, as above), to respect the remaining rights.

The next part of Hobbes's argument on rights is to say that not all rights are alienable. The rights to invade others and others' rights to invade us, which pose a threat to our preservation, are transferred and abandoned under the second law of nature but Hobbes is quick to say that while many rights can be transferred or abandoned, there are some that must never be given up. ". . . there be some Rights, which no man can be understood by any words, or other signes, to have abandoned or transferred."[36] Our right to preserve ourselves cannot be given up; it is inalienable. We must hold onto our right to self-preservation, according to Hobbes, and carry it with us into the commonwealth. Our right to self-preservation is so important, so central to the political argument that it remains with each subject.

This connects to another part of the orthodoxy I have been discussing (that all Hobbesian rights for subjects are weak and ineffectual), which concerns the sovereign. If the Hobbesian sovereign is absolute, as most commentators believe he is, then, they argue, subjects cannot hold rights against him in any meaningful way. It was a common argument of the royalists,[37] during the period when Hobbes was writing, during and just after the English Civil War, that all subjects must give up all their natural rights to the king. More radical royalists such as the Divine Right theorist Robert Filmer argued that *all natural rights* were originally held by the king, to be distributed (or not) to subjects as he chose. Those commentators who argue that the rights of Hobbesian subjects are not genuine political rights, include the right to self-preservation as another example of a right, held by Hobbesian subjects (though this time not abandoned or transferred),[38] that is yet of no significance and offers no protection. And once again, it is often a Hohfeldian analysis, combined with assumptions about absolute sovereignty that allows them to make some sense of such a position. If the right to self-preservation (or the more limited right to self-defence) is a mere Hohfeldian liberty right (privilege), then it is a *bare freedom* only and implies no correlative duties on the part of any others, or as here, on the part of the sovereign, to respect the right. This aids the argument that the right to self-preservation in Hobbes's theory is of no benefit to subjects and no threat to the absolute power of the sovereign.

And so, it is possible to argue, using Hohfeld's liberty right, that despite Hobbes's great emphasis on the importance of the right to self-preservation and the necessity, as he sees it, that each individual holds onto that right rather than giving it up to the sovereign, despite all that, this right, is, in the end, worthless. It is certainly appropriate to ask the question whether Hobbes would have made the right to self-preservation so central to his political argument if he had intended it to be perceived as having no significance at all. So, are these commentators right when they say that the Hobbesian right to self-preservation is of no political significance?

The starting point for many commentators is the idea that if the sovereign is absolute then that precludes any political rights on the part of subjects.[39] This fits nicely with the notion that Hobbes cannot countenance *claim rights* for subjects held against the sovereign. Hobbes is clear, they argue, when he says that the sovereign does not owe any contractual duties to the subjects.[40] This is why, once again, the Hohfeldian analysis distorts the reading of Hobbes. On a Hohfeldian analysis, if the sovereign cannot owe directly correlated duties to the subjects, then the subjects cannot hold claim rights against the sovereign and if they cannot hold claim rights then (on the Hohfeldian reading) they cannot hold political rights or indeed, rights that are of any value to subjects. But, in Hobbes's theory, the sovereign does have duties to the subjects, albeit not contractual duties towards individual subjects. These duties are set out when Hobbes describes the office of sovereign. "The OFFICE of the Soveraign (be it a Monarch, or an Assembly), consisteth in the end, for which he was trusted with the Soveraign Power, namely the procuration of *the safety of the people*; to which he is obliged by the Law of Nature."[41] And Hobbes then makes the point that when he says "safety of the people" he does not mean bare physical survival. "But by Safety here, is not meant a bare Preservation, but also all other Contentments of life, which every man by lawfull Industry, without danger of hurt to the Commonwealth, shall acquire to himself."[42]

This makes it clear that for Hobbes the right to self-preservation is much more than the bare self-defence right some commentators take it to be. Hobbes also makes clear the serious political consequences if the sovereign cannot or will not protect the people and ensure their safety. Next to the squib in which Hobbes says, "In what Cases Subjects are absolved of their obedience to their Soveraign," he declares that, '[t]he Obligation of Subjects to the Soveraign, is understood to last as long, and no longer, than the power lasteth, by which he is able to protect them." And he continues, "The end of Obedience is Protection; which, wheresoever a man seeth it, either in his own or in anothers sword, Nature applyeth his obedience to it, and his endeavour to maintaine it."[43] So, the sovereign's right to rule is dependent upon his ability and willingness to protect the subjects. And the subjects' rights to self-preservation are protected (indirectly, one might say), by the sovereign's duties to protect the people and ensure their safety etc. So, here we have subjects' rights being given a kind of protection that cannot be recognised within a Hohfeldian analysis because there are not directly correlated duties owed by the sovereign to individual subjects. Yet the end result is that the subjects' rights to self-preservation do get protected, in some sense, by the duties of the sovereign to protect them. I argue that the Hohfeldian reading, once again, distorts the picture, allowing commentators to argue that the right to self-preservation, is of no significance or value to subjects.

One notable exception to commentators (who use a Hohfeldian approach) underestimating the significance of the right to self-preservation, is Jean Hampton. For Hampton, the right to self-defence that is retained by subjects in the commonwealth is so strong that it "renders the entire Hobbesian justification for absolute sovereignty invalid."[44] Hampton starts by defining the right to self-preservation as narrowly as possible. "So let us begin by defining the right very narrowly as the privilege or liberty of defending one's body if it is attacked, or to do what is necessary to procure the means (e.g. food and shelter) to assure bodily survival."[45] By granting this admittedly narrow right to self-defence, Hampton argues, Hobbes is opening the door to the subjects to make their own judgements about whether or not to obey the sovereign. "If we accept this very natural interpretation of the self-defence right, then isn't this granting the subjects the right of private judgement concerning whether or not their lives are endangered?"[46] Once this private judgement is allowed, Hampton argues, the sovereign cannot be absolute. She argues that Hobbes, in Chapter 21 of *Leviathan* goes on to broaden the self-defence right into "the entire right to preserve oneself" and therefore "makes the subjects the judges of whether or not they will obey *any* of the sovereign's laws."[47]

Hampton takes the argument in a different direction from me but demonstrates that the subjects' right to self-preservation is of great political significance within the theory. Her conclusions differ from mine in that she argues that Hobbes's entire argument for absolute sovereignty fails. What she cannot see, because of her Hohfeldian interpretation, is that the sovereign's duties will (in some sense) protect the subjects' right to self-preservation. I argue that the right to self-preservation starts out as a simple liberty right, held under the aggregate "right of nature" but then changes after the institution of a sovereign, who takes on the duties of the office of sovereign, and becomes (indirectly) protected by those duties. So, it does not become a claim right in Hohfeldian terms, but it does become, in some sense, a protected right.

My conclusion is that the application of the Hohfeldian analysis of rights to Hobbes's political theory in *Leviathan*, has resulted in a distorted, inaccurate picture of Hobbes's theory of rights. Hobbesian subjects are said to have only liberty rights and no claim rights. Yet, Hobbes (in *Leviathan*) does clearly describe rights for subjects, held against each other, that are protected by the duties of others, after conforming to the second law of nature,[48] (and once a sovereign is instituted the laws of nature will be made actual laws, providing further protection). The unprotected rights of the state of nature; (rights that Hobbes himself says are of no good to anyone and offer no protections), have now surely become rights with some protections. And the unacceptable rights to invade and attack others, which are included under the "right to every thing, even to one anothers body" of the right of nature, are gone, replaced by "so much liberty against other men, as he would allow other men against himself."[49] But, according to the Hohfeldian analysis, such a thing is not possible and so the unprotected liberty rights of the state of nature must carry on through the process of conforming to the laws of nature, instituting a sovereign and entering a commonwealth and the duties Hobbes describes to respect the rights transferred, must be dismissed as meaningless.

Similarly, the aggregate liberty right to self-preservation, held under the right of nature, changes to become a protected right once the sovereign is instituted and takes on the duty of the office of sovereign to protect the people. The changes in the rights held by subjects from unprotected liberties (rights) to protected liberties (rights) cannot be explained using the Hohfeldian analysis. Commentators are restricted by the Hohfeldian definitions and so the picture of Hobbesian rights becomes distorted.

It is worth mentioning an alternative view of Hobbesian rights represented in an older tradition of Hobbes scholarship that also has its contemporary supporters. This tradition sees Hobbes as a natural law theorist or natural rights theorist.[50] This seems a reasonable possibility to consider, given that when Hobbes was writing, natural law was the dominant moral theory as well as legal theory and all discussions of subjective rights for individuals were discussed within the context of natural rights and natural law. Hobbes is certainly not a conventional natural law theorist however, and so some strenuous arguments are required to make the case that he is, in some sense, proposing a theory of natural law, despite his theory lacking many of the assumptions of a classical theory of natural law. Some scholars argue explicitly that Hobbes is an *unconventional* natural law theorist; Sharon Lloyd for example, argues that he proposes a "self-effacing natural law theory."[51] For our purposes, however, it is Hobbes's position on individual *rights* that must remain the focus. Many of those who see Hobbes as a natural law theorist also take the view that the theory of rights is weak.

One notable exception to this is Leo Strauss, who, whilst rejecting the characterisation of Hobbes as a *natural law* theorist, picks him out as having moved the argument from *natural law* to the *rights* of the individual. As I pointed out in chapter 2, Strauss famously dubbed Hobbes the "father of modern political philosophy" for emphasising the importance of the *rights* of individuals over the *obligations* of natural law.

> For it is he who, with a clarity never previously and never subsequently attained, made the "right of nature," i.e. the justified claims (of the individual) the basis of political philosophy, without any inconsistent borrowing from natural or divine law.[52]

Strauss recognised what others have failed to see; that Hobbes puts the rights of the individual at the centre of his political theory and that arguably this picks him out ahead even of Locke in the claim to be "the founder of modern political philosophy." "[H]e sought to prove the State as primarily founded on 'right' of which law is a mere consequence."[53]

Another writer who makes similar observations about Hobbes's theory in the historical context of natural law theory and the move to seeing the rights of the individual as central is A. P. d'Entrèves in his 1939 book *Natural Law: An Introduction to Legal Philosophy*[54] I also discussed his views in chapter 2 and so I will not say much here except to include the following quotation.

> The modern theory of natural law was not, properly speaking, a theory of law at all. It was a theory of rights. A momentous change has taken place under cover of the same verbal expressions. The *ius naturale* of the modern political philosopher is no longer the *lex naturalis* of the medieval moralist nor the *ius naturale* of the Roman lawyer. . . . As Hobbes pointed out with his usual shrewdness: "though they that speak of this subject use to confound *ius* and *lex*, *right* and *law*, yet they ought to be distinguished; because RIGHT consisteth in liberty to do, or to forbear: so that law and right differ as much, as obligation and liberty." (Lev. Ch 14)[55]

These writers see something in Hobbes's approach to the rights of the subjects that more recent commentators are unable to see through their Hohfeldian lens. (And commentators also fail to see it because of preconceptions about absolutism). They recognise the significance and the centrality of the individual rights, particularly the right to self-preservation that drive

Hobbes's political argument and provide the reason for individuals to agree to enter a commonwealth. They also recognise a move away from natural law thinking and towards something much more modern, focussed on the individual and her subjective rights rather than her obligations under natural law. The shortcomings of the Hohfeldian analysis of legal rights when applied to discussions of historical figures raise more questions about the implications of the use of Hohfeld's analysis in recent and current rights theorising, which will be addressed in the next chapter.

NOTES

1. A John Simmons, *The Lockean Theory of Rights* (Princeton: Princeton University Press, 1992), 70/71.

2. Simmons, *The Lockean Theory of Rights*, 71.

3. Simmons, *The Lockean Theory of Rights*, 71.

4. Simmons, *The Lockean Theory of Rights*, 70, n.11.

5. Simmons, *The Lockean Theory of Rights*, 70/71, n.12.

6. "the rights and liberties conceded by God and nature." William of Ockham, quoted in Brian Tierney, "The Idea of Natural Rights-Origins and Persistence," *Northwest Journal of International Human Rights* 1 (2004): 92.

7. Richard Tuck, *Natural Rights Theories, Their Origin and Development* (Cambridge: Cambridge University Press, 1979), 26.

8. Jean Gerson, quoted in Tuck, *Natural Rights Theories, Their Origin and Development*, 26/27.

9. Tierney, *"The Idea of Natural Rights-Origins and Persistence,"* 11.

10. Hugo Grotius, *The Rights of War and Peace*, transl. A. C. Campbell (2005, Adamant Media Corporation), unabridged facsimile of (Washington and London: M. Walter Dunne, 1901), 19–21.

11. John Locke, *Second Treatise of Government* [1690], ed. C. B. Macpherson (Indianapolis: Hacket Publishing Company, 1980), 9.

12. Hohfeld, *Fundamental Legal Conceptions* (New Haven: Yale University Press, 1919), 36.

13. See, for example, Cohen 1998, Finkelstein 2001, Gauthier 1969, Hampton 1986, Sreedhar 2010 and Kavka 1986, though Kavka renames a liberty right a "permission" right, emphasising, as does Sreedhar, that a liberty right signifies moral permissibility rather than claims or entitlements.

14. See, for example, Condren 2000, Gauthier 1969, Hampton 1986, Ryan 1996, Sreedhar 2010, Warrender 1957.

15. Susanne Sreedhar, *Hobbes on Resistance: Defying the Leviathan* (Cambridge: Cambridge University Press, 2010), 26/27.

16. Jean Hampton, *Hobbes and the Social Contract Tradition* (Cambridge: Cambridge University Press, 1986).

17. Hampton, *Hobbes and the Social Contract Tradition*, 51/52.

18. Gregory Kavka, *Hobbesian Moral and Political Theory* (Princeton: Princeton University Press, 1986).

19. Wesley Hohfeld, *Fundamental Legal Conceptions,* ed. Walter Wheeler Cook, Foreword by Arthur L. Corbin (1919) (Clark, NJ: The Lawbook Exchange Ltd., 2010).

20. Hohfeld, *Fundamental Legal Conceptions*, 38/39.

21. Mathew Kramer, "Rights Without Trimmings" in *A Debate Over Rights,* eds. Kramer, Simmonds and Steiner (Oxford: Oxford University Press, 1998), 8.

22. Waldron J. "The Role of Rights in Practical Reasoning: 'Rights' versus 'needs,'" *The Journal of Ethics* 4 (2009): 118.

23. Thomas Hobbes, *Leviathan* (1651), ed. C. B. Macpherson (London: Pelican book, 1968), 189.

24. Hobbes, Leviathan, 189.

25. Hobbes, *Leviathan*, 190.

26. Hobbes, *Leviathan*, 190.

27. Hobbes, *Leviathan*, 189.

28. Hobbes, *Leviathan*, 190.

29. Hobbes, *Leviathan*, 191.

30. Hobbes, *Leviathan*, 191.

31. Hobbes, *Leviathan*, 190/191.

32. Hampton, for example, says, "is Hobbes saying in this passage . . . that after renouncing a liberty-right, we have a duty to others, correlated with a claim-right that they have over us, to the effect that we do not try to exercise the liberty we have renounced? It certainly sounds like it . . ." Hampton, *Hobbes and The Social Contract Tradition*, 55. She then goes on to argue that although it sounds as though he is introducing claim-rights, he couldn't be because his subjectivist ethical theory doesn't allow for such moral obligations.

33. Hohfeld, *Fundamental Legal Conceptions*, 1919, Simmonds, 2002.

34. For the full version of the argument concerning the inalienable right to self-preservation and the duty of the sovereign to protect the people, see Eleanor Curran, "Can Rights Curb the Hobbesian Sovereign? The Full Right to Self-Preservation, Duties of sovereignty and the Limitations of Hohfeld," *Law and Philosophy* 25 (2006): 243–265.

35. "A LAW OF NATURE (*Lex Naturalis*), is a Precept, or generall Rule found out by Reason, by which a man is forbidden to do, that, which is destructive of his life, or taketh away the means of preserving the same; and omit, that, by which he thinketh it may be best preserved." Hobbes, *Leviathan*, 189.

36. Hobbes, *Leviathan*, 192.

37. See chapter 1.

38. In Chapter Fourteen Hobbes says, "And therefore there be some Rights, which no man can be understood by any signes, to have abandoned, or transferred. As first a man cannot lay down the right of resisting them, that assault him by force, to take away his life. . . . The same be sayd of Wounds and Chayns, and Imprisonment"; Hobbes, *Leviathan*, 192. Then, in Chapter Twenty One, he says, "[i]f the Soveraign command a man (though justly condemned,) to kill wound, or mayme himself; or not to resist those that assault him; or to abstain from the use of food, ayre, medicine, or any other thing, without which he cannot live; yet have that man the liberty to disobey." Hobbes, *Leviathan*, 268/269.

39. See, for example, Will Kymlicka, *Contemporary Political Philosophy* (Oxford: Clarendon Press, 1990), 130, ". . . as Hobbes puts it, there is a 'power irresistible' on earth, and for Hobbes and his contemporary followers, such power 'all actions really and properly, in whomsoever it is found.' *No one could claim rights of self-ownership against such power*" (my italics).

40. ". . . Because the right of bearing the Person of them all, is given to him they make Soveraigne, by Covenant onely of one to another, and not of him to any of them; there can happen no breach of Covenant on the part of the Soveraigne"; Hobbes, *Leviathan*, 230.

41. Hobbes, *Leviathan*, 376.

42. Hobbes, *Leviathan*, 376.

43. Hobbes, *Leviathan*, 272.

44. Hampton, *Hobbes and the Social Contract Tradition*, 197.

45. Hampton, *Hobbes and the Social Contract Tradition*, 198/199.

46. Hampton, *Hobbes and the Social Contract Tradition*, 199.

47. Hampton, *Hobbes and the Social Contract Tradition*, 201

48. "And when a man hath in either manner abandoned, or granted away his Right; then is he said to be OBLIGED, or BOUND, not to hinder those, to whom such Right is granted, or abandoned, from the benefit of it," Hobbes, *Leviathan*, 191.

49. Hobbes, *Leviathan*, 190.

50. Bobbio 1993, d'Entreves 1951, Murphy 1994, Lloyd 2001, Tuck 1979, Warrender 1957, Strauss 1936.

51. S. A. Lloyd, *Morality in the Philosophy of Thomas Hobbes: Cases in the Law of Nature* (Cambridge: Cambridge University Press, 2009).

52. Leo Strauss, *The Political Philosophy of Hobbes, Its Basis and Its Genesis*, transl. Elsa M Sinclair (1936) (Chicago: The University of Chicago Press, 1952) Midway reprint 1984, 156.

53. Strauss, *The Political Philosophy of Hobbes*, 157.

54. A. P. d'Entreves, *Natural Law, An Introduction to Legal Philosophy* (London: Hutchinson and co. (*Publishers*) Ltd., 1951).

55. d'Entreves, *Natural Law*, 59.

Part II

CURRENT AND FUTURE RIGHTS THEORY

ASSESSING THE PHILOSOPHY OF RIGHTS

Chapter 6

The Continuing Dominance of Hohfeld

As I have argued in previous chapters, the Hohfeldian approach to rights, by which I mean an acceptance not only of his analytical scheme but also his stipulation that only the claim-right is a right properly so called; that approach, when applied to moral and political rights, has some significant limitations and gives rise to some problems. The limitations may be summarised as: (1) putting a restriction on the duties that might protect rights, by making them strictly correlative to each individual right; (2) separating the notion of liberty from the notion of a right; and (3) failing to provide any content or value within the concept of a right. The problems this gives rise to may be summarised as: (1) a failure to account for rights that may be protected in other ways than by directly correlated duties attached to each right, (2) an inability to account for the fact that most rights theorists put forward the notion of *liberty* as an important concept attached to or as part of that of a right or in the form of an important "right to liberty," and (3) a failure to capture anything substantive or unique about the notion of a right that gives it its normative significance as something distinct from the duties that it may imply.

Followers of Hohfeld may argue that none of these limitations give rise to problems in rights theorising as the Hohfeldian scheme is merely doing what it sets out to do, that is, providing stipulative definitions of the four incidents and the legal relationships they imply. And, as I have said, I am not arguing against the Hohfeldian scheme as an accurate account of these legal incidents and relations. My concern is with the applicability of the scheme to theorising moral and political rights and Hohfeld's choice of the claim right as the only right properly so called.

This latter point is critical, both for illustrating the Hohfeldian position and for providing a critique of it. Hohfeld is emphatic that each incident of right provides a definition of a specific and singular form of legal relation (between at least two people) and that each relation, so described, picks out something quite distinct and precise. An important question for those applying Hohfeld's analysis to moral and political rights must be; is it appropriate to apply this understanding of the meaning of legal relations described by the term "right" to moral and political rights?

QUESTIONING THE APPLICATION OF HOHFELD'S SCHEME TO MORAL AND POLITICAL RIGHTS

In the last chapter I made the case that the acceptance and application of Hohfeld's analysis has led to a distorted reading of some historical writing on (moral/political) rights. In this chapter I will make the case that there are reasons why we should question the wholesale application of Hohfeld's scheme to modern theorising of moral and political rights.

If one were to ask how work on the theory of rights has developed or changed since the middle of the twentieth century one would have to acknowledge four things. First, the Hohfeldian analysis is generally accepted and continues to dominate thinking on rights; second, following the jurisprudential turn in rights theorising, two theories of rights, from within jurisprudence, dominate discussions, namely, interest theories and will theories and these discussions are often within a context of acceptance of the Hohfeldian analysis. The third focus for discussions concerns the *justification* of rights within a *moral* theory. These discussions provide justifications of rights either from deontological moral theories (now often termed "status theories") or from consequentialist moral theories (now often termed "instrumental theories"). I will not address these issues of pure moral philosophy here. And finally, the fourth development can be found in recent work in the field of theorising *human rights* and I will turn to that in the next chapter. In this chapter I will concentrate on the continuing influence of Hohfeld and offer three arguments concerning what I see as reasons against the wholesale application of the Hohfeldian analysis to moral and political theorising of individual rights.

As I pointed out in chapter 4, it is important to make a distinction between genuine *theories of rights* and Hohfeld's *analysis of legal rights* which stops well short of a fully fledged theory. A theory of rights must at least explain what a right is and what work it does and, if it is to include justification, then it must be set out within the context of a moral or political or legal theory or at least with some moral, political or jurisprudential justification. Clearly, Hohfeld's scheme does not do this, as it provides only stipulative definitions of four conceptions or "incidents" of the term "right" as used in the legal literature and the legal relationships implied by each of them.

Despite the fact that Hohfeld does not propose a *theory of rights*, his analysis is often accepted as foundational for understanding what rights are, to the extent that reference to an additional *theory* of rights is deemed unnecessary. On the other hand, there is also much rights theorising that *combines* either *will* or *interest* theory with a strict adherence to Hohfeld's analysis.[1] So, there are also *theories* of rights during this period; with the *will* and *interest* theories being the most discussed. Moral and political philosophers addressing the subject of rights have sometimes argued that rights are really just the "other side" of duties, with *duty* therefore being the primary moral concept and rights existing as correlatives of some duties. As Howard Warrender puts it "rights are merely the shadows cast by duties."[2] This view precludes the need for a specific theory of rights beyond whatever moral theory is being supported that includes a concept of duty that, in turn, supports the concept of rights. The notion that rights are just the other side of duties, has strong resonances in Hohfeld's "claim right" and has also continued its influence in philosophical discussions of rights by writers such as Onora O'Neill.[3]

The Hohfeldian analysis significantly influences discussions of rights from the middle of the twentieth century and continues that influence today. This is the case whether those discussions are within the context of legal rights, moral rights, or political rights. (There are some exceptions and some important work in rights theory that is anti-Hohfeldian, for example, the interest theories of both Raz and MacCormick). Some writing, which I will discuss below, has opened up discussion and some criticism of Hohfeld's analysis, but the majority of philosophical discussions of rights accept and rely upon the Hohfeldian definitions. What is more, they see the Hohfeldian analysis as providing the logical rock bottom of our understanding of rights and what they imply in relation to others. The perceived strength of the analysis regarding the relations between the various legal positions described is such that to question it is to risk being accused of misunderstanding the analysis. The four incidents and their legal opposites and correlatives are regarded by many as beyond criticism. To question them would be to commit a logical mistake. As I mentioned above, there has been important recent work developing philosophical justifications of *human rights,* which has taken rights theorising back to the realm of moral and political philosophy. Even this work, however, often sees the Hohfeldian analysis as being of central importance.[4]

It might be useful to start with a couple of discussions of moral rights where Hohfeld's scheme is questioned. There are examples of writers who criticise aspects of the Hohfeldian scheme but generally there is acceptance of the definitions themselves and of Hohfeld's declaration that it is only the legal relation described by a claim and its correlative duty "which is most properly called a right."[5] One notable exception is L. W. Sumner in his 1987 book, *The Moral Foundation of Rights,* which makes some substantive criticisms of Hohfeld's analysis. He also develops his own philosophical justification of rights by adopting a particular kind of consequentialist moral theory. Even Sumner, however, despite his criticisms, says that his work "remains Hohfeldian in spirit and inspiration."[6]

He starts by acknowledging the importance of Hohfeld to the field but with a hint of the critique to come. "Where analysis of rights is concerned, the beginning of wisdom, though not the end, lies in Wesley Hohfeld's celebrated classification of 'fundamental legal conceptions.'"[7] He continues,

> [d]espite its many virtues, however, Hohfeld's analytical work suffers from a number of limitations of its own. While many of these are matters of relatively insignificant detail . . . some require mention at the outset. To a philosopher's eye the most obvious of them is Hohfeld's failure to analyse any of his conceptions.[8]

There is recognition here that Hohfeld's stipulative definitions of the four incidents lack something, one might say, in philosophical depth or explanation. Sumner then goes on to make a substantive criticism concerning Hohfeld's insistence that it is only the claim right that is properly called a right.

> If the first limitation of Hohfeld's analysis lies in its lack of a systematic basic vocabulary, the second lies in one of its principal conclusions. Hohfeld contended that a right "in the strictest sense" or in its "limited and proper meaning" was itself one of his "fundamental conceptions," namely the correlative of a duty owed to some second party. He was therefore committed to holding (1) that the notion of a legal right has but one strict or proper sense and (2) that this sense is (in his scheme) atomic rather than molecular in its structure. Each of these contentions is, however, dubitable.[9]

I agree that Hohfeld is committed to holding (1) and with Sumner's conclusion that we should not interpret this as "a report about the actual state of judicial reasoning" which, as he rightly points out, is contradicted by Hohfeld's own complaints about the way "right" is actually used in the literature. Rather, Sumner says, we should interpret it as "a stipulation, as it was doubtless intended." And if it is a stipulation then "Hohfeld provided virtually no argument in favour of it."[10] I agree and I shall make my own argument about this below.

Regarding (2), Hohfeld's analysis includes many examples of rights that are a combination of two or more of his incidents, such as property rights, so, while the scheme is atomic in structure, his narrative demonstrates that the atomic elements can be close together in complex bundles of rights. Hohfeld himself gives the example of X who owns land, where "X has a *right* or *claim* that Y, the other man, should stay off the land, he himself has the *privilege* of entering on the land; or, in equivalent words, X does not have a duty to stay off."[11] We should note, however, that this takes nothing from Hohfeld's insistence that it is only the claim right—the right that Y should stay off the land—that can properly be called a right. What we can say, perhaps, is that the legal situation of X regarding his ownership of the land, and the various legal relations that gives rise to, is molecular and complex rather than atomic and simple.

As an illustration of such combinations of rights we might consider the rights connected to my walking on the common. I have a liberty right to walk on the common. It seems to me that Hohfeld is clear that there is such a (legal) right and it applies when I am free to do something (i.e., I have no obligation not to do it), but no one else has any duties correlative to that right to allow me to do it; to stand out of my way so that I may do it. All other people also have a liberty right to walk on the common and so none have a duty to stay off the common to allow my walk. Indeed, if the common is crowded with people, making use of their exercise time, and it is difficult for me to walk down the path without getting close to other people, then they still have no duty (in terms of their right to walk there) to stand back and allow me to take the path. They do have a duty, however, under rules of social distancing, to stay two metres away from me, because under rules of social distancing all people have a duty to stay two metres away from others and a correlative right that others stay two metres away from them. The duties and rights under rules of social distancing do not affect the liberty right that I have to walk on the common in the first place. (Although they would if such rules had forbidden walking on the common.) And so, as I walk down the path and other people approach on the same path, my liberty right to walk there does not oblige them to get out of my way but my claim right to social distance does oblige them to keep two metres away.

Sumner also draws attention to the limitations of Hohfeld's analysis because of its specific focus on legal rights. Hohfeld, he says, "was concerned solely with legal rights . . . Hohfeld's distinctions among types of legal conceptions presuppose logically prior distinctions among types of legal rules and are unintelligible except against this background." He goes on, "we will have to expand Hohfeld's narrow focus on rights within a municipal legal system to include rights within any conventional system, legal or non-legal."[12] Again, I agree, although I will suggest an approach that is more distinct from Hohfeld's than that which Sumner is proposing.

As I mentioned above, while Sumner does make substantive criticisms of Hohfeld, his approach remains broadly Hohfeldian, albeit with a few changes to the analysis.

Hohfeld's analytical framework will not serve our purposes as it stands. Thus what follows should be construed not as an explication of that framework but rather as a reconstruction of it which departs from Hohfeld on many issues of terminology, methodology, and substance. For all these departures, however, it retains and supports a great many of Hohfeld's contentions, including his basic commitment to two independent sets of conceptions, the members of each of which are connected by logical relations of contradiction and equivalence. More than that, however, it remains Hohfeldian in spirit and inspiration, since it shares Hohfeld's conviction that the nature of rights can be illuminated only by developing and deploying a clearly articulated normative vocabulary.[13]

Other writers accept the Hohfeldian system as it is and apply it to their own theorising on rights. Joel Feinberg, in his 1973 book, poses the question for legal rights "what is the difference between being *at liberty* to do (omit, have, or be) something and having a *right* to do (etc.) it?'[14] It seems he has already accepted both the Hohfeldian distinction between *liberty rights* (privileges) and *claim rights* and Hohfeld's declaration that the only right "properly so called" is a claim right. He refers directly to Hohfeld saying that he is "the classic source for the analysis of legal relations into rights, liberties, powers, and immunities"[15] before saying that legal writers such as Hohfeld "commonly distinguish '"rights in a strict and narrow sense," usually called *claim-rights*, from "mere liberties," often called *privileges* and sometimes *licenses*."[16]

Feinberg develops his own view in the context of the Hohfeldian definitional scheme. After saying that "many philosophical writers have simply identified rights with claims" he says "we shall see, a right is a kind of claim"[17] but he wants to investigate exactly what *kind* of claim might constitute a right. His analysis proceeds by examining the way that the language of rights and claims is used. He says that "claiming is an elaborate sort of rule governed activity" and that by looking at "the whole activity of claiming, which is public, familiar and open to our observation . . . we may learn more about the generic nature of rights than we could ever hope to learn from a formal definition."[18] It is interesting to note both the empirical methodology and the notion that rights are real social entities with their own "generic nature."

Feinberg settles on a "valid claim" as his preferred definition of a legal right and applies the same reasoning to understanding moral rights. "A man has a legal right when the official recognition of his claim (as valid) is called for by the governing rules. . . . A man has a moral right when he has a claim, the recognition of which is called for—not (necessarily) by legal rules—but by moral principles, or the principles of an enlightened conscience."[19] There are two things worth noting about this definition of a moral right. First, it relies heavily on the notion of a "claim" as the defining notion and second, it specifies no moral content beyond the vague assertion that the "claim" is "called for by moral principles." It is hard to see how this goes beyond the problematic (circular) formal definition he started with of a right as a claim and a claim as a right. We might say that, according to Feinberg, a moral right is a claim that would be acknowledged as valid according to some idea of morality. Feinberg does say, however, that there is not always direct correlativity between rights (claims) and duties and the most interesting example he offers is that arising from those he calls the "manifesto writers" by which he means those who wrote the American Declaration of Independence (1776), the Virginia Bill of Rights (1775), and the French Declaration of the Rights of Man and of Citizens (1789). As already discussed in chapter 1 , these writers were, of course, writing about "natural rights" and therefore had quite a different understanding of rights from the paired down Hohfeldian notion that Feinberg is working with. He admits, though, that he feels "a certain sympathy with the manifesto writers" and that he accepts "the moral principle that to have an unfulfilled need is to have a kind of claim against the world, even if against no one in particular."[20] He says that he is "even willing to speak of a special 'manifesto sense' of 'right,' in which a right need not be correlated with another's duty."[21] This is the sense of right, just mentioned, according to which a right is a claim *to something* which need not be a claim *against anyone in particular.*[22]

This is an important acknowledgement that goes some way towards recognising a weakness in the correlativity thesis that is so fundamental to the Hohfeldian analysis. Feinberg stops short of accepting that unfulfilled basic human needs might directly give rise to rights however, preferring to categorise them as "the natural seed from which rights grow." He allows such claims to "human rights" as "a valid exercise of rhetorical license."[23] They cannot be actual rights unless and until they conform to his definition of "valid claims."

It would take far too long to list all the sources of support for the Hohfeldian analysis in late twentieth century writing on rights, but one significant work is worth mentioning as an example. In their important 1998 book, *A Debate Over Rights*,[24] jurisprudes Mathew Kramer and Nigel Simmonds and political philosopher Hillel Steiner take issue over the finer points of analytical rights theorising. They debate extensively the merits or otherwise of the will and interest theories of rights but, as Kramer says in the introduction, "there are some methodological and substantive points that are common to the three essays—the most notable of which is an adherence to the framework of jural and deontic logic developed by Wesley Hohfeld."[25] Or, as Steiner puts it more colorfully, "the authors of this volume all worship at the temple of Hohfeld and share his attitude."[26]

If we move forward to the twenty first century, the Hohfeldian analysis is still very much at the forefront of theoretical work on rights. A recent collection of essays edited by Mark McBride continues the debate about rights using Hohfeld's analysis as a starting point and consciously carries on the discussion started by Kramer et al.[27] "Most significantly, in both this and the 1998 book, all contributors adopt the analytical framework of Wesley Hohfeld as a means to bring clarity of exposition to their espoused positions. They use Hohfeld's logical framework to articulate and defend their theories and also to critique the theories of others."[28]

ARGUMENTS AGAINST THE APPLICATION
OF THE HOHFELDIAN ANALYSIS TO
MORAL AND POLITICAL RIGHTS

It is important, at the start, to be clear about the *project* that Hohfeld was undertaking and its context. The first sentence of the first of the two essays that make up Hohfeld's *Fundamental Legal Conceptions* states, "[f]rom very early days down to the present time the essential nature of trusts and other equitable interests has formed a favourite subject for analysis and disputation."[29] After mentioning several distinguished legal theorists from Bacon[30] and Coke in the seventeenth century down to A. N. Whitlock in the early twentieth century, Hohfeld declares, "[i]t is believed that all of the discussions and analyses referred to are inadequate."[31] And in reply to those who may think that his interests in such discussions are rather esoteric he says, "[o]n the contrary, . . . the main purpose of the writer is to emphasize certain oft-neglected matters that may aid in the understanding and in the solution of practical, everyday problems of the law."[32] To this end, he says, he will discuss "as of chief concern, the basic conceptions of the law."[33] To do this he points out that, "[o]ne of the greatest hindrances to the clear understanding, the incisive statement, and the true solution of legal problems frequently arises from the express or tacit assumption that all legal relations may be reduced to 'rights' and 'duties' and that these latter categories are therefore adequate for the purpose of analysing even the most complex legal interests, such as trusts, options, escrows, 'future' interests, corporate interests, etc."[34]

It is common of course to see the law as bestowing rights and duties on those subject to it and to see legal relations as being between those with legal rights on the one hand and those with legal duties pertaining to those rights on the other. But what Hohfeld seems to be getting at here is to say that despite the term "right" being used loosely and generally, it can be broken down into four different meanings or legal positions, each describing a specific legal advantage and each with its own legal correlative and legal opposite. He illustrates this with the table below which he says illustrates "the strictly fundamental legal relations."[35]

Table 6.1 Hohfeld, *Fundamental Legal Conceptions*, 36

Jural Opposites	right	privilege	power	immunity
	No-right	duty	disability	liability
Jural Correlatives	right	privilege	power	Immunity
	duty	no-right	liability	disability

The passage following the table is greatly significant. "As already intimated, the term 'rights' tends to be used indiscriminately to cover what in a given case may be a privilege, a power or an immunity, rather than a right in the strictest sense."[36] Hohfeld is arguing, first that *loose talk* about legal positions and legal relations has led to different legal positions and relations being treated as though they are the same, that is, as though they are all simply rights and duties. Second, he is arguing that the differences between the four "incidents" are illustrated by their distinct legal correlatives and opposites.

One might ask the following question. If all of the four "incidents" are commonly described as "rights," then on what grounds does Hohfeld pick out his "right" or "claim" as the one that describes a "right in the strictest sense?" Surprisingly, Hohfeld returns to the "ordinary legal discourse" of which he has been so critical, to tell us that the "clue lies in the correlative 'duty,' for it is certain that even those who use the word and the conception 'right' in the broadest possible way are accustomed to thinking of 'duty' as the invariable correlative."[37] So, even those who are, in his view, mistakenly using the term "right" too broadly, do get one thing right, when they see "duty" as the correlative of "right" even when that is also a mistake if they are in fact, referring to a privilege, power or immunity, each of which, according to Hohfeld, has a different correlative. I am not being deliberately obtuse here, as I realise that when Hohfeld is read he is taken to be saying that in some sense there is a general understanding that a right is correlated with a duty, but I am pointing out that this does not fit easily with what he is arguing regarding the different incidents or conceptions as set out in the table where he goes against the "common understanding" of what a (legal) right is.

One might also point to an inconsistency in this argument, given his previous criticism of "looseness of usage." Presumably, what he means is that even those who use the term "right" too loosely or broadly, think that a right always implies a correlative duty. Given his previous point, however, that commentators apply the word "right" where it cannot be accurately used, this seems rather inconsistent. He seems to be saying both that one cannot rely on ordinary usage and that ordinary usage tells us what the correct correlative is. My quarrel is not with the four "incidents" that describe distinct legal relations but with Hohfeld's ascription of a special status to one of those incidents or conceptions, namely, his "right" or "claim" as "that legal relation which is most properly called a right or claim."[38] The same term, he says, which describes a right in "the strictest sense,"[39] giving the term its "limited and proper meaning."[40]

What can Hohfeld mean by this? He gives us no explanation. If he is, as he says, analysing the way the term "right" is used in the legal literature, in order to gain clarity for our legal understanding and to aid the pragmatic solving of legal problems, then his conclusions, illustrated in the table, demonstrate that there are four distinct ways in which the tern "right" is used in the law. Each of these four uses implies a distinct legal relation and each could be said to describe a *type of legal right*. When he then states that only one of the four, the "right" or "claim." is a right "in the strictest sense," he must be saying that there is justification for picking this one out as in some sense more truly a right than the other incidents (which are also referred to as rights in the legal literature). He does not give us any content or value that attaches to this particular notion of a right, that does not attach to the others (unless one could count being correlated with a legal duty as a value in itself which seems doubtful). So, why does he not just say that there are four distinct kinds of legal rights, with their own correlatives and opposites, but they are all, equally, rights? The only argument he provides is that, as above, everyone who uses the term "right," including those who use it too broadly, agree on one thing and that is, that a right is correlated with a duty on the part of at least one other person. He seems to be saying that all genuine rights are correlated with a duty on the part of at least one other person. There is something about having a correlative duty that marks the claim out as a right "properly so called."

It is hard not to draw the conclusion that Hohfeld is stepping beyond the boundaries of his stated project of merely analysing the use of the term "right" in the legal literature, to make a claim about *what can count as a genuine right* and what cannot. Why, for example, can a privilege or liberty not count as a genuine right? In ordinary usage liberties are often said to be rights even with the restricted meaning Hohfeld gives to "privilege" with its correlative "no-right." In his own example, as above, where X has a right that Y stay off his land, with the correlative that "Y is under a duty to stay off the place," X also "has the *privilege* of entering on the land";[41] so, we might say X has *a right* to enter his own land. Hohfeld reiterates that this privilege means that X does not have a duty to stay off, so it is the opposite of a duty and he also reminds us that the correlative of X's privilege to enter the land is "Y's 'no-right' "that X shall not enter."[42] Hohfeld is making clear the distinction between a *right or claim* and a *privilege or liberty* and I have no argument with that or with the distinct legal relations implied by each but what is less clear, I argue, is what his justification is for declaring that of these two types of legal right only the *claim* is "a right in the strictest sense." Putting such qualms aside, I shall move on to my own arguments.

I want to make three rather simple arguments in support of my objection to the wholesale application of the Hohfeldian scheme to moral and political rights. The first argument against the blanket use of Hohfeld concerns the separation of *rights* (claims) from *liberties* (privileges) that is an inevitable consequence of applying his analysis. Hohfeld's conceptions wrench apart the notions of *right* and *liberty*, which were so closely aligned historically, in *natural rights* theories and more recently, in the form of many discussions of the importance of *the right to liberty*.[43]

Rights (claims) are Distinct from Liberties (privileges)

In Hohfeld's scheme of legal conceptions and relations, the relations implied by "privilege" or "liberty right" are of particular importance and relevance to moral and political rights. The reason for this is that the notion of privilege (or liberty), of being "free" to do something or not do something has been an important and significant notion historically, in discussions of *natural rights* and down to the present day, in discussions of moral and political rights.

My right to walk on my land is a liberty right and distinct from my claim right that you stay off. Hohfeld's position is that there is a logical distinction between the different incidents of right. He gives the following example:

> The eating of a shrimp salad is an interest of mine, and if I can pay for it, the law will protect that interest, and it is therefore a right of mine to eat shrimp salad which I have paid for, although I know that shrimp salad always gives me colic.

And he then defines the rights involved,

> [t[his passage seems to suggest primarily two classes of relations: *first*, the party's respective privileges, as against A, B, C, D and others in relation to eating the salad, or, correlatively, the respective 'no-rights' of A, B, C, D and others that the party should not eat the salad; *second*, the party's respective rights (or claims) as against A, B, C, D and others that they should not interfere with the physical act of eating the salad, or, correlatively, the respective duties of A, B, C, D and others that they should not interfere.[44]

And he adds, "These two groups of relations seem perfectly distinct; and the privileges could, in a given case, exist even though the rights mentioned did not."[45] In other words, each Hohfeldian category or "incident" is the type of right it is and nothing else. If it is a liberty right (privilege) it cannot have the characteristics of a claim right and if it is a claim right it cannot have the characteristics of a liberty right. As he says when describing the distinction between privileges (liberty rights) and claim rights,

The importance of keeping the conception of a right (or claim) and the conception of a privilege quite distinct from each other seems evident; and, more than that, it is equally clear that there should be a separate term to represent the latter relation. No doubt, as already indicated, it is very common to use the term 'right' indiscriminately, even when the relation designated is really that of privilege; and only too often this identity of terms has involved . . . a confusion or blurring of ideas.[46]

This latter point is critical, both for illustrating the Hohfeldian position and for providing a critique of it. Hohfeld is emphatic that each incident of right provides a definition of a specific and singular form of legal relation (between at least two people) and that each relation, so described, picks out something quite distinct and precise. An important question for those applying Hohfeld's analysis to moral and political rights must be; is it appropriate to apply this understanding of legal relations described by the term "right" to moral and political rights?

From the start of his analysis, Hohfeld rids the notion of a *right* of any association with the notion of *liberty* and restricts (the notion of a) *right* to being no more than a *claim* to the duty of another/others. In the context of the legal relations that he is examining this makes sense. We can see that the legal relation which *implies a duty* on the part of at least one other is indeed quite distinct from the legal relation which *implies a "no-right"* on the part of at least one other and that the notion of a *claim* (to the duty of another) is quite distinct from the notion of *being free from a duty* (to do or not to do something etc.) When we are considering moral and political rights, however, the context is different.

This stripping out of the notion of liberty from that of a right has significance for the way we understand moral and political rights. If we apply Hohfeld's analysis, then a right cannot include an idea of liberty at its core, in the way that much early writing on *natural rights* includes such an idea. And it is not only in the work of *natural rights* theorists that the notion of liberty is strongly connected to that of a right. Many recent writers have recognised the importance of the idea of liberty to that of a right and some such as Mackie make direct reference to Hohfeld.[47] Others like Griffin include liberty as itself one of the "highest-level human rights."[48]

The influence of Hohfeld's analysis is such that many recent rights theorists do apply it wholesale to moral and political rights.[49] Some theorists, like Jeremy Waldron, strike a cautionary note,[50] but Waldron himself then goes on to say that the Hohfeldian *"claim-right* is generally regarded as coming closest to capturing the concept of individual rights used in political morality."[51] And Mathew Kramer declares that, "virtually every aspect of Hohfeld's analytical scheme applies as well, *mutatis mutandis*, to the structuring of moral relationships."[52] He goes on, "[a] right or claim, then is the legal position created through the imposing of a duty on someone else"[53] and he thinks that this also applies to moral claims (with the proviso that purely moral claims do not have a correlative duty which is in the end, enforceable by the state, in the way that legal claims do). To have a *liberty* to engage in an action, on the other hand, according to Kramer, "is to be free from any duty to eschew the action"; equally "a liberty to abstain from a certain action is to be free from any duty to undertake the action."[54] Kramer then points out that although, "[t]he person against whom the liberty is held has a no-right concerning the activity or state of affairs to which the liberty pertains," yet "although that person has no *right* to the halting of the activity or state of affairs, he himself may well have a *liberty* to interfere."[55] Here, Kramer is treating the *liberty to X* as something that should be stopped. Perhaps he is thinking of unjustified freedoms such as the liberty to take all the apples on a common, leaving none for others. This sort of example is not relevant for my argument as I am concerned with liberties that could be said to rights, which implies that they are justified. Kramer proceeds to argue, however, that liberties may also be *protected* even though they are not, on Hohfeld's account, *directly protected* in the form of correlative duties. They may be protected by the duties correlated with other rights held by the person with the liberty. "[o]ne's actions or inactions grounded in liberties are effectively protected—to a considerable extent—by rights that do not pertain specifically to those actions or inactions."[56] This example is relevant to my argument as he seems to be saying that some liberties should and can, albeit indirectly, be protected.

Kramer sticks with Hohfeld's scheme while seeking to demonstrate that liberties as well as claims can be protected, though not by directly correlated duties. It is interesting to note both that he wants to show that liberties can have protections, despite being definitionally excluded from protection by Hohfeld *and* that there are ways to offer protections that are not provided by directly correlated duties.

Hohfeld himself makes it clear that, in many situations, liberties (privileges) are closely aligned to claims and are indeed given some protection by the duties correlated to those closely aligned claims. In the example given above, of the landowner, his *liberty* to enter his land is to some extent protected by the duties pertaining to his *claim* that others stay off his land. Property rights, in other words, comprise complex combinations of claims and liberties.

This works well when we are talking about legal rights and the intricate legal relations that they give rise to. Does it work well for moral and political rights? One obvious example where it does not that is sometimes mentioned in the literature is Hobbes's theory of rights and specifically his "right of nature" (as discussed in some detail in chapter 5). Hobbes, of course, *defines* all rights as *liberties*. Kramer mentions it in relation to Hohfeld's liberties. In the previous passage he has argued that, as above, "liberties can be protected quite extensively even though the liberties do not themselves place restrictions on anyone."[57] He then says, "in almost every situation outside the Hobbesian state of nature, conduct in accordance with a liberty will receive at least a modicum of protection through a person's basic rights."[58]

In Hobbes's state of nature the liberties are, as discussed in chapter 5, "bare liberties," that is, freedoms with no protections. As I argued in that chapter, some of these liberties do become protected by the transfer and laying down of rights Hobbes describes under the second law of nature and the taking on of duties not to interfere with the transferred liberties. This leaves us with liberties that are protected by correlated duties. Hohfeld's definitions cannot account for these liberties (rights) that Hobbes describes, which become protected by duties owed to the right (liberty) holder. This is one example of a case where rights described in a theory of political rights cannot be accommodated by Hohfeld's scheme without distortion of the theory.

There is another important point to make regarding liberties in the context of political rights. In the legal context it makes sense to define a liberty simply as the opposite of a duty or as the lack of a duty. To be legally free to X is to lack any legal duty not to X. In the political context, however, it is different. To be *free to X* is also *to be able to X* because no one is preventing you from X ing. So, taking freedom of movement as an example of a political right; I have freedom of movement so long as no one (and in this case it will usually be the state), is preventing me from: moving across the country, leaving the country, walking down the street and so on. In this case my liberty to move freely about is protected by the state's guaranteed lack of interference. This protection is required in order for me to have this freedom. If the lack of interference is not assured then I cannot be said to have this liberty. This has been illustrated recently in observing the takeover of Afghanistan by the Taliban. Whereas, before the takeover, woman had freedom of movement, that is, their freedom to move about was guaranteed by the state's commitment not to interfere; now, that lack of interference is no longer guaranteed, indeed interference is clearly threatened and so women are much less visible on the street as their perception of their freedom of movement changes.

Hohfeld's definition of liberty or privilege is inadequate as a definition of liberty in a political context as it fails to account for the notion of being *free to X* as *being able to X due to non-interference*. It also fails because this kind of liberty needs to be correlated with the duties of others and particularly the duty of the state, not to interfere. In other words, it requires *protection* which the Hohfeldian liberty/privilege lacks. Kramer's solution, as above, that "in almost every situation outside the Hobbesian state of nature, conduct in accordance with a liberty will receive at least a modicum of protection through a person's basic rights," fails to work in the political context first, because it simply assumes that "basic rights" are in place and second, even if "basic rights" are in place the correlative duties to those rights such as perhaps not to assault someone will not prevent their freedom of movement being interfered with. They might be very gently prevented from proceeding to travel.

MUST THERE BE STRICT CORRELATIVITY OF RIGHTS AND DUTIES FOR MORAL AND POLITICAL RIGHTS?

The strict correlativity between rights and duties is one example of the way in which the Hohfeldian analysis illustrates the immutability of the legal relations it defines. Each legal conception is defined by the legal correlative and legal opposite it implies. So, a power is precisely that legal ability to affect and change the legal position of another and its inverse is the inability to do so. And, in Hohfeldian terms, its legal correlative is a *liability* to have one's legal position altered and its legal opposite, is the *disability* to affect the legal position of another. Similarly, a claim (right) is precisely that legal ability to demand performance of a legal duty by another/others and its inverse is no ability to demand such a duty. And, in Hohfeldian terms, a claim right's legal correlative is a *duty* to allow or uphold the claim and its legal opposite, is the *no-right* to demand such a duty.

Such a scheme of legal conceptions (all of which are often referred to in the legal literature as rights but more precisely described by Hohfeld's four separate conceptions), enables one to pick out the distinct legal relations that are implied by each one. This sort of scheme is very useful for analysing conceptions and relations within a legal system. I argue that it is not always applicable, however, to moral and political relations and conceptions.

Whether or not having a moral or political right *means* that one has a claim to someone else's duty is, I argue, open to question. For example, one could follow MacCormick and say that a right can be "prior to duty" rather than being just a "reflex" of a duty.[59] Or one could follow Raz and say that "a right is a ground for duties" and furthermore that "[m]any rights ground duties which fall short of securing their object, and they may ground many duties not one."[60]

He goes on to argue that "there is no closed list of duties which correspond to the right" and gives as an example the right to political participation which, he says, has created new duties in modern states that were not possible in the past such as "a duty on the government to make public its plans and proposals before a decision on them is reached," as well as "a duty to publish its reasons for a decision once reached (except in special categories of cases such as those involving defence secrets)." Raz refers to "this dynamic aspect of rights, their ability to create new duties," which he says is disregarded by "most if not all formulations of the correlativity thesis."[61] I would add to this that it is a particular characteristic of political rights, in contrast to legal rights, that they have this "dynamic aspect." While it is in the nature of legal rights that they must be capable of precise, binding definition and delimitation, theories of political rights are created in the context of discussion of political values and principles. Such values and principles are constantly debated and always open to change which then affects the rights they give rise to and the duties that might protect such rights. This is in addition to the sorts of societal changes Raz is talking about. He also uses the generic term "rights" and limits his description of the dynamism of rights to the creation of new duties, while I wish to specify moral and political rights and to extend the dynamic aspect to the notion of such rights to include duties held to others or to an office or role that then protect such rights indirectly. In other words, I would like to suggest an alternative possibility to rights having directly correlated duties. Some rights might be protected in other ways, for example, by duties other than those owed directly to the rightsholder.

I will turn to Hobbes again for my first example of a theory of political rights that includes rights that are protected by duties that are not held directly to the rightsholder. In *Leviathan* Hobbes describes the right of nature as an unprotected liberty to any and all actions that I deem necessary in order to preserve myself. As described in chapter 5, Hobbes says that those liberties which are dangerous to others must be given up or transferred and only those liberties we would be happy for others to hold against us are retained.[62] When we move into a commonwealth the remaining (aggregate) right to full self-preservation is still maintained[63] and once a sovereign is instituted it becomes protected by the duties of the sovereign to ensure the safety of the people.[64] These duties are not held directly to subjects but are duties of the office of sovereign. Despite the fact that these duties are not directly correlated to the rights of individuals or directly held to those individuals, the duties will, nevertheless, protect the right to self-preservation that is held by all subjects.

For my second example, I go back to Afghanistan and to the freedom of movement of women which was a right recognised and protected by the previous government. For an individual police officer going about his work, there was no need for him to have a duty to protect each woman's freedom of movement. He might well have strongly disagreed that women should have such a right. His duty lay in obeying his orders and his orders included protecting women's freedom of movement. As long as he obeyed his orders, then he would in fact be protecting women's right to free movement, without having such duties directly to the individual women. Now that the government is being run by the Taliban, the same fictional policeman might be receiving orders to restrict the movement of women and so will no longer be protecting their right to free movement, even though he is still carrying out his duties of employment.

Once one questions the strict correlativity between a right and the duty/duties that protect it/uphold it/provide it etc. then it ceases to be necessary to follow Hohfeld in saying, as above, that we must keep "the conception of a right (or claim) and the conception of a privilege quite distinct from each other."[65] This is because once we separate the notion of duty from that of right; it will cease to be contradictory to include the notion of liberty within that of a right. My final argument against the wholesale application of Hohfeld's scheme to moral and political rights concerns the question of values.

RIGHTS EXPRESS VALUES WITHIN A THEORY OF POLITICAL MORALITY

I argue that if we follow Hohfeld and accept the stipulation that his *claim* is the only right properly so called, then we are left with an impoverished conception of a right. It is a conception of a right that lacks, first, any connection to the notion of liberty, as discussed above, and second, any content at all, beyond its relationship to a duty. To have a right, then, is merely to be the recipient of someone else's duty. It lacks any association with moral or political *value,* beyond being related to duties. Even this relationship could be said to lack moral or political value because it is a relationship to *legal* duties which may not represent moral or political duties.

Moral and political rights connect to *values* within a theory of political morality. The theory must tell us both what rights are and why they are justified. If we try to justify the Hohfeldian claim right, we will have to do so in terms of the duty it implies as the claim itself means no more than an entitlement to that correlative duty. As Kramer argues, using Williams, there is no independently existing right, only the duty that the claim implies. Of course, it is possible to argue that this is indeed where the value of a right lies, in the duties that oblige us to protect it. And this position has a history in moral philosophy and continues today in the work of writers like Onora O'Neill.[66]

One of the consequences, however, of thinking of a right in this way, is that it diminishes the significance of the right itself, which exists only as the other side of the duty. If we look to duties to discover the rights that they imply, we also run the risk of having to include rights that are, at the least, counterintuitive. The right to be punished would be one such right. If it is the duty of the state to punish wrongdoing when it involves law breaking, then, on a Hohfeldian account, it would seem that were the state to fail in this duty it would violate a right to be punished on the part of the lawbreaker.

Historically, there have been arguments defending such a right, for example in the context of the enlightenment ideal of punishment according to rational norms, but the idea of such a right has not gained support more generally. Indeed, in a recent article it has been argued that such a "right" is unsustainable "from the standpoint of the two main theories of rights—the will and interest conceptions."[67]

Perhaps the most obvious historical example of a political theorist, who develops his theory of rights using notions of moral and political value, is Locke. It is easy to see the values that inform his notion of a right. Individuals have rights because they were created by God as equal and independent beings and endowed with reason which enables them to know the law of nature, or the moral law. It follows, according to Locke, that "being all *equal and independent,* no one ought to harm another in his life, health, liberty or possessions: . . . And that all men may be restrained from invading others rights."[68] He argues that "all men" are naturally in "*a state of perfect freedom* to order their actions, and dispose of their possessions and persons, as they think fit, within the bounds of the law of nature, without asking leave, or depending upon the will of any other man."[69] All these values—of liberty, equality, and independence, come, in this case, from Locke's theological assumptions and inform and underpin his development of a theory of natural rights. The theological assumptions also provide (in the historical context) unassailable moral authority for the theory.

These Lockean values and the (theory of) natural rights they give rise to, are discernibly present in the documents of the French and American Revolutions and the Bills of Rights they inspire. The same Lockean values and notions of natural rights but without the theological premises are also present in the foundational human rights documents written after the Second World War. My argument has been that with the jurisprudential turn in rights theorising, the understanding of individual rights; what exactly they are, and what they do, has changed significantly. And whilst one could argue that, at least in the legal field, that understanding has become more technically accurate, thanks to Hohfeld; one could also argue, that in terms of moral and political values that might attach to the idea of individual rights; these have been stripped away, leaving the Hohfeldian *claim right* as the exemplar of an individual right "in its limited and proper sense." Just as others have referred to liberty rights as "bare freedoms" one might refer to claim rights as "bare claims" with no content beyond the duties they imply. An important recent development in rights theorising has however, returned to questions of the moral and political values that inform and justify our notion of individual rights. There has been an explosion of work in the philosophy of human rights that I will explore in the next chapter. For the first part of that chapter I will briefly look again at the *Will* and *Interest* theories of rights. Many commentators who accept the Hohfeldian analysis of rights believe that either the *will* or the *interest* theory provide the content and explanation of rights that the Hohfeldian analysis leaves out.

NOTES

1. See, for example, Kramer, Simmonds and Steiner, *A Debate Over Rights* (Oxford: Oxford University Press, 1998) and Mark McBride ed., *New Essays on the Nature of Rights* (Oxford: Hart Publishing, 2017).

2. Howard Warrender, *The Political Philosophy of Hobbes: His Theory of Obligation* (Oxford: Clarendon Press, 1957),

> A "right" as the term is generally used in moral and political philosophy, means something to which one is morally entitled. In this sense, it is used as a comprehensive description of the duties of other people towards oneself in some particular respect. . . . The rights-formula, therefore, is a loose, summarising expression that might be useful in an argument where others are denying this right . . . but, as a vehicle of philosophical enquiry, it is insignificant. (p. 18)

3. Onora O'Neill, "without obligation there are no rights" (as quoted in chapter 4) from "The Dark Side of Human Rights," *International Affairs* 81, no. 2 (2005): 431. See also, O'Neill, *Toward Justice and Virtue: A Constructive Account of Practical Reasoning* (Cambridge: Cambridge University Press, 1996) and O'Neill, *A Question of Trust* (Cambridge: Cambridge University Press, 2002).

4. See, for example, Carl Wellman, *The Moral Dimensions of Human Rights* (New York: Oxford University Press, 2011), v., "First, one should take legal rights as models of all species of rights, including moral rights. Second, one should analyze the content of any human right in terms of Hohfeld's fundamental legal conceptions or their moral analogues."

5. Wesley Hohfeld, *Fundamental Legal Conceptions: As Applied in Judicial Reasoning* (Clark, NJ: The Lawbook Exchange Ltd., 2010), 39.

6. L. W. Sumner, *The Moral Foundation of Rights* (Oxford: Oxford University Press, 1984), 21.

7. Sumner, *The Moral Foundation of Rights*, 18.

8. Sumner, *The Moral Foundation of Rights*, 18/19.

9. Sumner, *The Moral Foundation of Rights*, 19.

10. Sumner, *The Moral Foundation of Rights*, 19.

11. Hohfeld, *Fundamental Legal Conceptions*, 39.

12. Sumner, *The Moral Foundation of Rights*, 20.

13. Sumner, *The Moral Foundation of Rights*, 20/21.

14. Joel Feinberg, *Social Philosophy* (Englewood Cliffs, NJ: Prentice-Hall Inc., 1973), 55.

15. Feinberg, *Social Philosophy*, 56, n. 1.

16. Feinberg, *Social Philosophy*, 56.

17. Feinberg, *Social Philosophy*, 64.

18. Feinberg, *Social Philosophy*, 64. He has already noted that formal definitions of rights are inclined to become circular—"rights are claims, claims are rights."

19. Feinberg, *Social Philosophy*, 67.

20. Feinberg, *Social Philosophy*, 67.

21. Feinberg, *Social Philosophy*, 67.

22. There has been a great deal of discussion of whether Hohfeld's analysis can allow for rights held *in rem* or "against the world" as well as rights held *in personam*. See for example, Kramer, in Kramer, Simmonds and Steiner, *A Debate over Rights*, 9, n. 2.

23. Feinberg, *Social Philosophy*, 67.

24. Kramer, Simmonds and Steiner, *A Debate over Rights*.

25. Kramer, Simmonds and Steiner, *A Debate over Rights*, 2.

26. Kramer, Simmonds and Steiner, *A Debate over Rights*, 234.

27. McBride ed., *New Essays on the Nature of Rights*.

28. Mcbride ed., *New Essay on the Nature of Rights*, xi.

29. Hohfeld, *Fundamental Legal Conceptions*, 23.

30. From Bacon he quotes, "The nature of an use is best discerned by considering what it is not, and then what it is. . . . First, an use is no right, title, or interest in law; and therefore master attorney, who read upon this statute, said well, that there are but two rights: *Jus in re: Jus ad rem*" (circa, 1602; Rowe's ed., 1806), quoted in Hohfeld, *Fundamental legal Conceptions*, 23.

31. Hohfeld, *Fundamental legal Conceptions*, 25.

32. Hohfeld, *Fundamental legal Conceptions*, 26.

33. Hohfeld, *Fundamental legal Conceptions*, 7.

34. Hohfeld, *Fundamental legal Conceptions*, 35.

35. Hohfeld, *Fundamental legal Conceptions*, 36.

36. Hohfeld, *Fundamental legal Conceptions*, 36.

37. Hohfeld, *Fundamental legal Conceptions*, 38.

38. Hohfeld, *Fundamental legal Conceptions*, 39.

39. Hohfeld, *Fundamental legal Conceptions*, 36.

40. Hohfeld, *Fundamental legal Conceptions* 38.

41. Hohfeld, *Fundamental legal Conceptions*, 38.

42. Hohfeld, *Fundamental legal Conceptions*, 39.

43. Perhaps most famously in H. L. A. Hart's "Are There Any Natural rights?" in Jeremy Waldron's *Theories of Rights* (Oxford: Oxford University Press, 1984), 7. The first sentence reads, "I shall advance the thesis that if there any moral rights at all, it follows that there is at least one natural right, the equal right of all men to be free."

44. Hohfeld, *Fundamental Legal Conceptions*, 41.

45. Hohfeld, *Fundamental Legal Conceptions*, 41.

46. Hohfeld, *Fundamental Legal Conceptions*, 39.

47. "A right in the most important sense, is the conjunction of a freedom and a claim-right." J. L. Mackie, "Can there be a Right-based Moral Theory?" in Waldron ed., *Theories of Rights*, 169.

48. "All human rights will then come under one or another of these three over-arching headings: autonomy, welfare, and liberty. And those three can be seen as

constituting a trio of highest-level human rights." James Griffin, *On Human Rights* (Oxford: Oxford University Press, 2008), 149.

49. See n iv above for quotation from Carl Wellman, *The Moral Dimensions of Human Rights* (New York: Oxford University Press, 2011).

50. "We need to recognize that when we apply the Hohfeldian analysis in the moral sphere, we must expect claims about moral rights to reflect the vagueness and indeterminacy afflicting claims about moral duty and obligation in general." Waldron ed., *Theories of Rights*, 8.

51. Waldron, ed., *Theories of Rights*, 8.

52. Kramer, in Kramer, Simmonds and Steiner, *A Debate over Rights*, 8.

53. Kramer, in Kramer, Simmonds and Steiner, *A Debate over Rights*, 9.

54. Kramer, in Kramer, Simmonds and Steiner, *A Debate over Rights*, 9.

55. Kramer, in Kramer, Simmonds and Steiner, *A Debate over Rights*, 9.

56. Kramer, in Kramer, Simmonds and Steiner, *A Debate over Rights*, 11/12.

57. Kramer, in Kramer, Simmonds and Steiner, *A Debate over Rights*, 11.

58. Kramer, in Kramer, Simmonds and Steiner, *A Debate over Rights*, 12.

59. D. N. MacCormick, "Rights in Legislation," in *Law, Morality and Society, Essays in honour of H. L. A. Hart*, eds. P. M. S. Hacker and J. Raz (Oxford: Oxford University Press, 1977), 201.

60. Joseph Raz, *The Morality of Freedom* (Oxford: Oxford University Press, 1986), 170/171.

61. Raz, *The Morality of Freedom*, 171.

62. Hobbes, *Leviathan*, 190/191.

63. "As it is necessary for all men to that seek peace, to lay down certain Rights of Nature; that is to say, not to have libertie to do all they list: so it is necessary for mans life to retain some; as right to governe their owne bodies; enjoy aire, water, motion, waies to go from place to place; and all things else without which a man cannot live, or not live well." Hobbes, *Leviathan*, 211/212.

64. "The OFFICE of the Soveraign . . . consisteth in the end, for which he was trusted with the Soveraign Power, namely the procuration of *the safety of the people*," Hobbes, *Leviathan*, 376.

65. Hohfeld, *Fundamental Legal Conceptions*, 39.

66. ONora O'Neill, *Toward Justice and Virtue: A Constructive Account of Practical Reasoning* (Cambridge: Cambridge University Press, 1996), *A Question of Trust* (BBC *Reith Lecture*, 2002), "Response to John Tasioulas," in *Philosophical Foundations of Human Rights*, eds. Cruft, Liao and Renzo (New York: Oxford University Press, 2015).

67. "The right to be punished is shown to be largely indefensible on both counts: on the will theory, the right to be punished conflicts with autonomy . . . on the interest theory, a perpetrator's interest in punishment, inasmuch as it exists, is not sufficient to ground a duty on the part of the state." Adriana Placani and Stearns Broadhead, "Right to be Punished?" in the *European Journal of Analytic Philosophy* 16, no. 1 (2020): 53–74.

68. Locke, ed., C. B. Macpherson, *Second Treatise of Government* [1690] (Indianapolis: Hackett Publishing company Inc., 1980), 9.

69. Locke, *Second Treatise of Government*, 8.

Chapter 7

Current Theories of Rights

The Will and Interest Theories and Theories of Human Rights

WILL AND INTEREST THEORIES

The *Will* and *Interest* theories of rights continue to dominate the headlines in rights theory. They can usefully be described, using Wenar's terminology, as being "theories of the function of rights,"[1] as they describe what rights do for those who hold them; though one could also say that they each provide a justificatory ground for rights, namely in human interests or in human agency or "will." Each theory provides criteria that must be met for something to qualify as a right and as such, both are subject to counterexamples and objections because of, either generally accepted "rights" that fail to qualify, or the extension of the notion of a right to examples that most would not consider to be justified. This means that neither theory can be said to have fully succeeded in providing a satisfactory account of what a right is.

I will briefly address the objections to both theories that I have already mentioned in chapter 4. Each theory clearly captures something important about how we might understand what a right is and what it does and yet both fall foul of counterexamples. The counterexamples to the will theory are particularly striking as they appear to demonstrate that the theory cannot accommodate some rights that are generally thought to be of great importance and significance, such as children's rights, the rights of unconscious patients and inalienable rights. It *defines* rights in terms of the power of the right-holder over the duty implied by the right and so it cannot accept any rights attached to right-holders who lack the necessary capacity to exercise that power over the duty-bearer or any rights where the duty cannot be waived for other reasons, such as inalienability. According to the theory, the right-holder must be capable of and in a position to, either waive the duty or insist on its performance. This stipulation rules out all people who lack capacity, from children and minors to unconscious patients and those with severe mental disabilities as well as also failing to allow for inalienable rights. If I cannot alienate my right to life by telling you it is ok for you to kill me (in other words, by waiving your duty not to kill me), then I do not have the necessary control over the duty implied by my right to life and consequently, there is no right to life, understood as an inalienable right, on the will theory.

The will theory undeniably captures an important notion that rights reflect agency and the ability of individuals to assert themselves in the world. When I declare, "I have a right to X" I am asserting some sort of a claim on my own behalf. Never-the-less, the will theory, by making the right-holder's *control* (over the correlated duty) the *key* to holding a right, fails to account for some of the most important individual rights (as above) that are recognized in any typical list of human rights or moral and political rights. The theory therefore can be said to fail to fully explain what a right is.

The interest theory does not suffer from a similarly long list of important rights that it cannot accommodate and yet it too fails to account for all rights and also leads in some cases to a proliferation of rights beyond accepted limits. If a right exists when the imposing of a corresponding duty on others would serve the interests of the right-holder then we are led to an extension of rights to those whom we do not normally consider to hold them. These would include, for example, all those who would benefit if I was paid back a loan that I have made to X. Clearly, I have a right to be repaid the loan by X, and I have an interest in being paid back and will benefit from being paid back but many others could also benefit from the repayment. I may use the money to pay some bills, buy my friend dinner and put a deposit on a holiday house. All the recipients of these payments have an interest in the loan being repaid and will benefit from its repayment, yet we do not think that they have a *right* to the repayment of the loan. This is an example of the *third party beneficiaries* objection which has generated much recent discussion in attempts either to resolve it and defend interest theory,[2] or to show that it cannot be resolved and therefore defeats interest theory.[3] Raz's version of interest theory, which defines the interests that generate rights as those which represent *well-being,* reduces the amount of possible third part beneficiary objections and this version also goes some way further towards a notion that fits more comfortably with moral and political rights.[4] Even this version runs into problems however. It might increase X's well-being to be better paid than all his colleagues, but this does not give X a *right* to be better paid than all his colleagues. While it may be the case that the notion of well-being is an important one when we are thinking about what rights are, or when they are generated, it is not specific enough to limit cases of rights in a convincing way.

Just as significant perhaps, for the interest theory, are the counterexamples that arise from the contrary objection that there are people who have particular rights (often attached to being an office holder or having a particular role) who do not have an interest or sufficient interest to categorize it as a right according to the interest theory. If I make you the executor of my will, you will then have certain rights as executor that you may well not regard as being in your interests or to your benefit to hold.

Recent work on rights theory has seen attempts to provide a modern *hybrid theory*[5] that tries to resolve the problems of counterexamples by including elements from both the interest and will theories and other new theories such as Wenar's *kind-desire* theory of claim-rights[6] and McBride's *tracking* theory (influenced by Sreenivasan's hybrid theory).[7] Sreenivasan's theory rather ingeniously shows that the objection to will theory regarding inalienable rights can be solved if we grant that the reason for saying that right-holders should be in control of the correlative duty is because that control (usually) advances their interests. He is then able to argue that, in certain cases (such as the inalienable right not to be enslaved), the right-holder's interests are advanced by *not* having the control and not being able to waive the duty. He is also able, on the same reasoning, to get around the common third part beneficiary objection to interest theory (as I have outlined above in the case of the promise to pay back a loan). In this case, it can be said of those people who are not directly promised the repayment of the loan but will benefit from its repayment that they are not in a position to waive the duty as no duty is owed directly to them. But in this case their interests are *not* advanced by *not having the power* to waive the duty.[8]

Wenar's kind-desire theory sets out to provide an analysis of rights that "will capture all the rights assertions we make—not only within morality and law, for example, but within sports and games and etiquette. . . . In short, a good analysis will make sense of all the ways we speak of rights."[9] He argues that his kind-desire theory achieves this and also deals with all the counterexamples that arise from the will and interest theories. "KIND-DESIRE THEORY: some system of norms refers to entities under descriptions that are kinds ("parent," "journalist," "human," etc.). Within such a system, claim-rights correspond to those enforceable strict duties that members of the relevant kind want to be fulfilled."[10] The weight of the definition of a claim-right is on the desire, "the want," although there must be reason for the desire, given the particular kind in question. Wenar argues that the kind-desire theory can defeat objections raised against the will theory regarding children and the comatose who are incapable of waiving duties. "Our duties to young children not to abuse them correlate with rights in those young children not to be abused, because young children (like everyone, or perhaps even more than others) have reason to want not to be abused. And the same, mutatis mutandis, for the comatose."[11] If by this he means that the young child and the comatose patient have reasons which lead them to desire not to be abused, this seems unconvincing. If he means that we can assign reasons to them for not wanting to be abused, it is hard to understand what could be meant by a desire that someone would have reason to hold if they were capable of (1) understanding the reasons and (2) actually having the desire. At first glance it seems that the comatose patient can have neither (1) nor (2) and the child might have (2) but probably won't have (1) (depending on age and ability).

MOVING BEYOND THE IMPASSE

An important point to take away from the ongoing and seemingly endless debate between the will and interest theories (and now including the new hybrid theory and other new theories as above), is that it is hard to see what might resolve the disputes, despite much skilled manoeuvring by those on all sides. There is an impasse certainly between the will and interest theories, because neither "side" is likely to give up their favoured notion of what characterizes a right. It is easy to agree that both theories do capture something important or even essential about how we understand the notion of a right. The difficulty comes with the project of finding a way of reducing our understanding of what a right is to one core characteristic that will capture all rights and exclude all non-rights. When the rights under discussion include all legal rights, as well as moral and political rights, social rights, human rights and so on, it is of course extremely difficult if not impossible to come up with such a characteristic. The new hybrid theory suffers from being vulnerable to the attack that it merely combines the two competing theories.

In conclusion, the most striking aspect of the debate and the continuous claim and counter claim is that none of the meticulously constructed defences and attacks succeeds in decisively resolving the issues. At the heart of the dispute is a fundamental disagreement about what is at the core of a right. Is it human agency? Is it the power to put someone under a duty (and equally to be able to choose to release someone from that duty)? Or is it human interests? Is it human need or human well-being that generates the claims to protection that we sometimes call rights? It is significant perhaps that, if one has a *legal* right one has the power to hold others under a duty and if that duty is not performed one has the power to demand redress; while in the context of moral and political rights, it may well be the case that the person with the right has no such power and indeed is in a weak and vulnerable position. In such cases, the protection of the right, if the protection is to be enacted, is more likely to come from others who recognize a need, rather than from the right-holder exercising a power. It could be argued that even if weak and vulnerable, the right-holder is still owed a correlative (moral/political) duty but the lack of power to bring about performance of the duty shifts the emphasis, in trying to explain the right, away from the notion that it is always the right-holder that has that power.

It is possible that attempts to reduce the analysis of rights to one core notion of what generates a right are doomed to suffer from counterexamples and objections as long as they are trying to account for all forms of right in their analysis. In the next section I will examine a new burst of rights theorising that may herald a return to the consideration of universal moral rights.

FINDING VALUE IN RIGHTS
THEORY—HUMAN RIGHTS

I made the point in the last chapter that the Hohfeldian notion of a claim (right) has no connection to moral or political *value* (except indirectly through the correlated duty) and that such value is required if the claim right is to be taken as defining moral and political rights as well as legal rights. Some might object that the Hohfeldian analysis provides only stipulative definitions in "a framework of jural and deontic logic,"[12] or that it describes only the "form" of rights,[13] and not their justification or that moral or political *value* can be supplied by additional reference to theories of rights and/or to moral theories. But none of this undermines the point that the Hohfeldian definitions restrict what can be said about rights that might connect them to moral or political value. For example, Hobbesian rights which are all defined as liberties, cannot be accommodated within the Hohfeldian analysis (except, as shown in chapter 5, by misreading all Hobbesian rights as Hohfeldian liberty rights). As well as lacking value, the Hohfeldian claim right restricts our notion of a right both in terms of the direct and strict correlativity to duties it imposes and in its separation from the notion of liberty.

The next question for this chapter, is whether anything can be found in recent work on the philosophy of *human rights* that would address or get around these problems? At first glance it seems that we have moved from a dearth to a surfeit. Recent theorising about human rights is full of references to values, particularly when suggesting possible grounding concepts for human rights. These can be put into a list containing at least the following contenders: human well-being, fundamental human interests, human needs, agency, normative agency, autonomy, liberty, dignity, fairness, equality, and positive freedom. One could say that at least two of these; interests and agency mirror the values captured in the interest and will theories of rights, respectively. It is not surprising, perhaps, that there is a certain amount of overlap between attempts to provide theories of rights within jurisprudence and the attempts to provide theories of rights, focusing on human rights. What is distinctive about recent attempts to theorize *human rights,* however, is the move away from jurisprudence and theories that set out to include all forms of legal rights as well as moral and political rights, to more narrowly focused theories that only include human rights (although, of course, human rights are often protected in international or domestic law, so theories of human rights do sometimes directly address those specific legal protections). This switch to *human rights,* moves rights theorising to the contemplation of rights that are universal and apply to all human being simply by virtue of their humanity.[14] Human rights clearly have strong echoes of *natural rights.*

The idea of *human rights* is often said to come from that of *natural rights,*[15] as it takes the same starting point: that all human beings have certain rights just by virtue of being human. This universality of human rights, along with the notion of their inviolability and of applying at all times and in all places, whether or not they are protected by law, makes the idea of human rights sound very close to that of natural rights. One obvious difference is the lack of theological premises. God is missing from human rights documents and from most discussions of human rights. Appeals to natural law and to human reason as providing knowledge of natural law are also missing, with the exception of some Catholic philosophy. In the early years after the first human rights documents, we had the interesting situation of a doctrine of universal individual rights, which was accepted as having great moral and political significance by a great many people and yet which had no obvious or stated philosophical foundation other than the consensus after the Second World War that the atrocities committed during that war must not be repeated. The United Nations Charter and the Universal Declaration of Human Rights both echo earlier documents such as the American Declaration of Independence, in their natural rights language, though without reference to God. "WE THE PEOPLES OF THE UNITED NATIONS DETERMINED . . . to reaffirm faith in fundamental human rights, in the dignity and worth of the human person, in the equal rights of men and women and of nations large and small."[16] As Carl Wellman says, "the United Nations Charter presupposes the existence of fundamental rights that are grounded on the dignity and worth of the human person rather than on any social institutions. In that sense and in that sense only, they are natural rather than artificial rights."[17]

One thing that I want to emphasize because I think it is significant is that the burgeoning literature on the philosophical foundations of *human rights* brings rights theorising back to the subject matter of *natural rights.* The significance of this is that it was the early natural rights theorists, such as the Spanish writers defending the rights of Indigenous peoples under Spanish colonial rule in the sixteenth century and the theorists of the seventeenth century applying natural rights to theories of government, who developed a revolutionary idea. This was the idea that all people, no matter their social or political or legal status, hold certain fundamental rights and that these rights are inviolable and should be respected and protected.

The traditional notion of rights, on the other hand, was of advantageous positions held by particular people, as a matter of law or custom, where individuals or groups are owed what is said to be their *due*, according to those laws or customs. The right or the claim to have one's due, according to some status one has, as a property owner, or a ruler or a parent, is something that all societies recognize and enforce. The revolutionary idea, on the other hand; the idea that all human beings have *equal worth* or *value* or *dignity,* which accords them certain fundamental rights, is the one that was new in the late medieval and early modern periods. This revolutionary idea was increasingly explored within political theory by writers like Hobbes, and Locke and then enfolded into the revolutionary documents of the American and French revolutions. The idea takes hold in political discourse and practice, but study of its philosophical justification experiences a rupture in the wake of the attacks on natural rights and natural law by the new positivists,[18] and empiricists,[19] and the philosophical study of rights largely moves back into the realm of law and of legal and social organisation and jurisprudence. Rights theorising becomes dominated by jurisprudential discussions and this continues in much philosophical work on rights to the present day.

In this history of rights theorising that I am examining, the next interesting split, we might say, is between theorising about rights and the growing *practice* of *human rights* in the wake of the Second World War. While the *practice of human rights* continued to gain in importance and significance, becoming a central political and moral concern as well as becoming embedded in international and national law, its theoretical underpinning was largely ignored. Human rights were accepted as a sort of cleansed version of natural rights; they were natural rights without the unseemly theological and metaphysical baggage. When the attention of philosophers does finally turn to providing philosophical justification for the increasingly influential notion of human rights, we might expect it to mark a return to the ambit of *natural rights*, with its focus once again on the idea of certain fundamental rights held universally and equally by all humans, simply by virtue of their humanity. And we might equally expect this work to mark a departure from jurisprudential discussions and their dominance by the ultimate jurisprudential analysis of rights; the Hohfeldian scheme of legal relations.

The reality is, inevitably, more complex and nuanced than this. The new philosophers of human rights do indeed explore once again the possible justification of the notion of universal, inviolable (human) rights, held by all equally and many acknowledge that these rights are, first and foremost, *moral* rights as they exist beyond and before their legal protection. At the same time, however, many also refer to existing theories such as the interest and will theories and to the dominant Hohfeldian notion of all rights as claim rights with correlative duties and they often weave these notions into their new theories of human rights. Some more detail on these developments may be helpful.

In the decades following the first declarations of human rights there was little additional theoretical writing specifically on *human rights* and it is not until the latter part of the twentieth century that we start to see attempts to provide a theoretical underpinning for those rights set out in the documents and increasingly referred to in the law and in political discourse. The last third of the twentieth century sees the start of the philosophical examination of human rights in the work of writers like Alan Gewirth, Maurice Cranston, Joel Feinberg, Jack Donelly, James Nickel, and John Rawls,[20] and the work continues apace today.

Some theorists draw attention to the fact that human rights are part of international law and part of political practice, as well as being set out in the constitutions of many countries. This aspect of being part of the *practice* of international law and politics provides the starting point for some attempts to provide a theory or justification of human rights. One way of categorising theorists is to say that they can be roughly divided between those who focus on this aspect of human rights as *practice*[21] and those who focus on human rights as universal moral rights.[22] There are also those who focus on human rights as part of a theory of social or political justice.[23] Another useful way of characterising the different theories is by what grounding concept(s) they propose for human rights. These include: dignity and interests (Tasioulas 2015), agency and autonomy (Gewirth 1996, Griffin 2008), a good life (Nickel 2007, Liao 2015) basic human needs (Renzo 2015), and a combination of agency, needs, and good life.[24]

Recent theorists of human rights could be said to agree to the following:

1. The idea of human rights comes from that of *natural rights* as it developed out of traditional natural law theory. The idea of natural rights strengthened through the seventeenth and eighteenth centuries, culminating in the influential documents of the French and American revolutions, before losing credibility due to their theological and metaphysical assumptions. The revolutionary *idea*, however (that each person has rights that attach to them simply be virtue of the fact that they are human), lives on in the so called manifestoes and the documents of the United Nations and other international and national bodies.
2. This *idea,* of universal rights attaching to each human being, now renamed "human rights," is taken up after the Second World War in the documents of the United Nations and other international and national bodies. The references to God and objective natural law are replaced by secular, non-metaphysical language.

3. While the *idea* and *practice* of human rights has gained strength, its philosophical justification was neglected in the decades after the appearance of the initial human rights documents. The material facts of human rights laws and the efforts to enforce them have become an important reality of international law and politics. It is now important to provide philosophical analysis and justification of the notion of human rights.

Recent theorists *disagree,* however, on what specifically, *justifies* human rights and, sometimes, on what *characterizes* human rights. For example, some writers argue that human rights are always the other side of a duty, whether or not they explicitly subscribe to Hohfeld.[25] One can also loosely group recent theories of human rights, as above, into, those which ground human rights in human agency or autonomy of some form, those who ground them in human needs and those who ground them in well-being or a good life.

If human rights are universal, then whatever grounding is chosen must apply to all humans. This is where theories can run into problems. Taking agency or autonomy as the grounding concept, for example, raises the issue of those humans who cannot be said to have agency or autonomy, such as people in a vegetative state or new-born babies. It is generally thought that such humans do have human rights although some theorists bite the bullet and argue that not all humans have rights.[26] This also raises the old question of what it is that makes us uniquely human, sometimes accompanied by the assumption that it will be that thing that can ground human rights. Others ask what it is that makes human life uniquely valuable. And yet, however we answer these questions there will always be the further question, why that characteristic or value justifies conferring rights on all humans. If we are uniquely human because we are X, why does that then give us a *right to X*? We need a value or values combined with or as part of a moral theory to fully justify (1) our allocation of human rights to individuals and (2) the imposing of duties and responsibilities on others that will provide protection for such rights. Without the ultimate backing of the notion of humans having moral value, any justification for rights is open to a "so what?" objection. So, all humans are rational, why does that mean that they have rights that should be respected?

One way to proceed is to justify the rights by reference to a moral theory. Sumner, for example, uses utilitarianism (though speaking of rights generally rather than human rights specifically, he is however addressing *moral* rights), to provide a philosophical justification. Starting from a recognition that rights and consequentialism have often been seen as incompatible, Sumner sets out to argue against this orthodoxy.

The main theoretical conclusion to be defended in what follows is that the supposed incompatibility between commitment to a basic goal and acceptance of constraints on the pursuit of that goal is an illusion. Any viable form of consequentialism, when combined with a realistic picture of the nature of moral agents and of the world within which they operate, must make room for rights.[27]

Or, one can justify rights by reference to a deontological moral theory such as Kant's. It is easy to move from Kant's second formulation of the categorical imperative,[28] to an acceptance that all persons have a right to be treated with equal dignity and respect. As mentioned above, debates about justifying rights between these two classical moral theories are now often conducted in terms of "status" theories and "instrumental" theories. "Status" theories pick out that human characteristic or characteristics which give human beings a special status which makes them worthy of having rights. Or, put another way, such characteristics illustrate the fact that humans are fitting subjects for rights. Characteristics such as dignity, rationality, autonomy, free will, the ability to choose a good life are all argued to be such characteristics. The third possibility is to justify rights by contractarian theories, based on whatever principles of justice people would agree to under appropriate conditions. The fact that they would be agreed to is enough to give them the status of principles of justice.[29]

SUGGESTED GROUNDING CONCEPTS
FOR HUMAN RIGHTS

Agency/Autonomy

The notion of agency, or more precisely, "normative agency" is put forward by James Griffin. Griffin states that he wants to follow the spirit of the natural rights tradition in picking out what makes us uniquely human. "Human rights can then be seen as protections of our human standing."[30] His answer to the question of what we mean by a "distinctively *human* existence," is that "our status centres on our being agents,"[31] and terming our uniquely human status as "personhood" he then breaks down than notion into three components of agency: autonomy, "minimum provision" (of resources and capabilities) needed in order to act autonomously and liberty (to act without being "blocked" by others).[32] He also links this notion of agency to that of human dignity. "To adopt the personhood account of human rights is to adopt normative agency as the interpretation of "the dignity of the human person" when that phrase is used of the ground of human rights."[33]

As often happens with the recent exploration of the philosophy of human rights, an apparently straightforward and simple grounding concept starts to multiply until one has several grounding concepts, or, as here, one grounding concept, agency, is shown to have several "components" or requirements. So, according to Griffin, the notion of personhood (which defines our human status), comprises more than simple agency. It also includes a need for a minimum provision of resources, certain capabilities and liberty. This is not surprising perhaps, when we consider how many rights have to be covered by any theory of human rights. Any theory needs to show that it will provide justification for the full gamut of human rights. On the other hand, Griffin is also concerned that the notion of human rights itself "suffers from no small indeterminateness of sense."[34] He says that the historical notion of natural rights we inherited, once it lost its theological component, provided few criteria for deciding when it was or was not appropriately applied. He takes the view that what is needed is an account of human rights that will enable us to include all the rights that are accepted as human rights while also making the concept of human rights sufficiently determinate that we can clearly see its boundaries.

Griffin makes the case that human existence can be defined by agency and that agency has three components which he argues "can be seen as constituting a trio of highest-level human rights" of autonomy, liberty, and welfare.[35] In order to live with agency, one has to be capable of autonomy and to be capable of autonomy one needs a certain amount of liberty and a minimal level of welfare. This is to state Griffin's case rather crudely.

Alan Gewirth's argument for grounding human rights in agency and autonomy takes a different approach in trying show the logical necessity of a recognition that agency and autonomy are necessary goods for a human being. But it ends up in a similar place to Griffin, at least to the extent that he argues that the requirements for agency are freedom and well-being.[36]

Fundamental Interests and Dignity

"Human rights are rights that all humans possess simply in virtue of their humanity; on an interest-based account, they are rights grounded in universal interests that generate duties on the part of others."[37] John Tasioulas, defining an interest as something which, if fulfilled, enhances an aspect of someone's well-being, argues that the existence of a human right can be established if the right serves one or more basic interests (e.g. in health, physical security, autonomy, understanding, friendship, achievement, play), if that interest is of sufficient importance to justify imposing duties on others and if these duties are reasonable, all things considered. These conditions must apply to "all human beings within a historical context, and simply by virtue of their humanity.[38]" Tasioulas also ties his argument to the notion of human dignity. It is a presupposition of his "schema" "that human beings have the capacity to possess moral rights.[39] "And that capacity means we are beings who are an ultimate source of moral concern. Human dignity consists in an "equality of basic moral status." Tasioulas concludes by saying that human rights "are grounded in the universal interests of their holders, all of whom possess the equal moral status of human dignity. This is a two-level pluralist account of the grounding of human rights, since it appeals to both moral (equal human dignity) and prudential (universal human interests) considerations, and allows a plurality of human interests to play a grounding role."[40] It is worth noting the reference to the equal moral status of all human beings which features in traditional natural rights arguments such as Locke's.

Basic Needs

Massimo Renzo, in his account of human rights, first criticizes Griffin for identifying human dignity with agency because, he argues, this means that those humans, who lack agency, therefore lack human rights. When we say that X has a right not to be tortured, we mean that it is incompatible with our understanding of the respect due to X as a human being that we should allow X to be tortured. Griffin's argument, according to Renzo, fails to account for the fact that we generally understand human rights to be universal, applying to all human beings. Renzo puts forward "the notion of human needs" as "a better candidate for grounding our conception of humanity."[41] He also criticizes Griffin's account for being open to the objection of parochialism because by placing the status of ultimate human value as lying in agency, he ties it to western liberal societies, for whom agency and autonomy are ultimate human values but which may be rejected by other societies organized around different values such as community or tradition. Renzo's solution is to turn to the notion of human needs which applies to all.

> An adequate theory of human rights will thus have to provide a more inclusive account, one capable of accommodating our considered judgement that children, the severely mentally disabled, and individuals suffering from advanced dementia also possess human rights, while at the same time relying on some feature of humanity whose value cannot be reasonably rejected by non-liberal moralities. The best candidate, I will suggest, is the idea of human needs.[42]

He argues that while many of our needs arise from our desires—if you want to drive then you need a license—there are certain *basic needs* that must be met if we are to live "a minimally decent human life."[43] "It is on this notion that a plausible justification of human rights can be founded."[44]

Renzo addresses objections to a "basic needs" approach to justifying human rights that are raised by Griffin. First, the objection that using a basic needs approach will restrict too narrowly what can count as a human right. For example, the right to freedom of religion might not count as fulfilling a basic need as a life might be lived in a minimally decent way without this right. If a minimally decent life means healthy biologically and psychologically then this sets the bar too low. Renzo argues that the idea of a minimally decent life is richer than this and encompasses social needs as well, requiring social interaction and a minimal amount of recognition. This, he suggests, is what distinguishes human life from the life of other animals.[45] Renzo also responds to an objection from the opposite direction; that if a minimally decent life means meeting all physiological needs, then it will mean a right to every health need imaginable and this will make rights "implausibly lavish." Renzo responds to this objection by saying that it fails to recognize the limits implied by "*basic* needs" which will only cover those needs that must be met in order to live a minimally decent life.

Renzo raises another objection to the "basic needs" approach, which he thinks is the most serious objection to the account he is proposing and that is the objection that if it follows from his argument that anyone whose human rights are violated (say someone is raped or tortured) cannot be said to live a minimally decent life, then this undermines the "basic needs" approach to justifying human rights. His answer is to move from what he says has so far been an "instrumental account" which justifies human rights by arguing that they help us realise the goal of a minimally decent life, to a non-instrumental account which claims that human rights have non-instrumental value. "The idea is that these rights express the worth that human beings have as ends in themselves."[46] Now we seem to have a Kantian justification of human rights according to which, human rights ". . . embody a form of recognition of the value of each individual."[47] Asking himself whether this makes his "basic needs" approach redundant, Renzo replies by saying first, that one can combine an instrumental account with a non-instrumental account and that "a plausible justification of human rights is likely to be one that acknowledges the important role that both justifications play."[48] And second, that the notion of "basic needs" also figures within the non-instrumental account because basic needs "identify the sort of protections that if disrespected" produce the type of "moral injury to our status as human beings," that are referred to in the non-instrumental accounts of Nagel and Kamm. Renzo concludes that "[h]uman rights protect the conditions for a minimally decent life by providing us with the opportunity to meet such needs and by expressing the value we have *qua* human beings."[49]

A Good Life

James Nickel states that he will offer "a pluralistic justificatory framework for human rights" that will endorse "several kinds of justifications of human rights: (1) prudential arguments, that is, one's claiming that people will have better prospects for a good life when they live under a political system that recognises, respects, and protects their human rights; (2) utilitarian and pragmatic justifications; and (3) arguments from plausible moral norms and values, including fairness, dignity, minimal well-being, security, and liberty."[50]

Mathew Liao states that a substantive account of human rights can be given that shows that "human beings have human rights to what I call the fundamental conditions for pursuing a good life."[51] He characterizes a "good life" as "one spent in pursuing certain valuable, basic activities." "'Basic' activities are activities that are important to 'human beings qua human beings' life as a whole." And "[f]inally, basic activities are ones that if a human life did not involve the pursuit of any of them, then that life could not be a good life."[52] He gives as examples of basic activities, deep personal relationships, knowledge, active pleasures such as creative work and play and passive pleasures such as appreciating beauty.[53] Liao says that the contents of the fundamental conditions for pursuing a good life can be derived from these basic activities. Further, the fundamental conditions for pursuing a good life are "various goods, capacities, and options that human beings qua human beings need, whatever else they (qua individuals) might need, in order to *pursue* the basic activities."[54] The fundamental *goods* would include for example, what we need to sustain ourselves physically, such as food, water and air. The fundamental *capacities* are powers and abilities we need in order to pursue the basic activities and would include "the capacity to think, to be motivated by facts, to know, to choose an act freely (liberty), to appreciate the worth of something, to develop interpersonal relationships, and to have control of the direction of one's life (autonomy)."[55] And finally, the fundamental *options* are "those social forms and institutions required to exercise their essential capacities to engage in the basic activities."[56] These would include "the option to have social interaction, to acquire further knowledge, to evaluate and appreciate things, and to determine the direction of one's life."[57] Liao concludes, "In my view these fundamental conditions for pursuing a good life ground human rights because having these conditions is of fundamental importance to human beings and because rights can offer powerful protection to those who possess them."[58]

ASSESSING COMPETING ACCOUNTS OF
GROUNDING CONCEPTS FOR HUMAN RIGHTS

The first thing to note is that each of the above accounts of a grounding concept for human rights, starts with one, or in some cases two, grounding concepts but quickly proceeds to include many additional requirements, some of which could also be considered as "grounding concepts." Griffin, for example, in his argument for agency and dignity as grounding concepts, then argues that in order to have agency we need, autonomy, minimum provision, and liberty. And in describing our "status as human beings" or having human "standing" he also uses the notion of *personhood*. "One can break down the notion of personhood into clearer components by breaking down the notion of agency."[59] He says human rights should be primarily grounded in personhood but if personhood was the only ground it would leave "many human rights still too indeterminate."[60] He suggests a further or second ground of "practicalities." "Practicalities will be empirical information about . . . human nature and human societies, prominently about the limits of human understanding and motivation."[61] He then suggests a third ground, of equality. "The idea of human rights emerged with the growth of egalitarianism, and it is an obvious thought that equality is *a* or even *the*, ground for those rights."[62] He goes on, "[i]t is obvious that on one interpretation of 'equality'—namely, equal respect—and on one interpretation of 'grounds,' equality is indeed a ground for human rights."[63]

Renzo, in putting forward "basic needs" as his grounding concept, expands it to include everything that is required for a minimally decent life and then expands it again to include social as well as physical needs. Then, in defending his notion, he moves from an instrumental account to also include a non-instrumental account because "rights express the worth that human beings have as ends in themselves."[64]

Nickel, in proposing a "good life" as his grounding concept, states that he will propose "a pluralistic justificatory framework for human rights" that will endorse "several kinds of justifications of human rights."[65] These include justifications that are: prudential, utilitarian and pragmatic and arguments from moral norms and values including: fairness, dignity, minimal well-being, security, and liberty.

I need go no further for now. This is enough I think, to illustrate the point that finding a grounding concept for human rights can quickly become a very complex discussion that includes (what are perceived to be) many other important or vital concepts for human rights. Although each account starts from an apparently clear position that human rights are grounded in; needs, or agency or conceptions of a good life, each one moves to expand their grounding concept to include notions one associates with one or other of the other grounding concepts. So, agency expands to include "resources and capabilities" and also a minimal provision of welfare. "Basic needs" expands to include social needs that would include religious or spiritual needs and "a good life" expands to include fairness and dignity. As I mentioned above, this is, at least in part, driven by the need to make sure that all human rights are covered. The list of human rights is an expansive one of course and includes quite distinct sorts of rights which are often referred to in discussions as coming under the categories of either, "political and civil rights" or "social, economic, and cultural rights." Indeed, these distinctions are recognized when these rights are put forth separately in some of the official documents such as the International Covenant on Civil and Political rights and the International Covenant on Economic, Social and Cultural rights.

THE RELATIONSHIP OF HUMAN RIGHTS
THEORISTS TO HOHFELD

The second question to ask about these theories is whether the human rights theorists accept and adopt a Hohfeldian approach to the analysis of rights. The short answer is that some do but, interestingly, many do not. This needs to be qualified though, with the observation that while many human rights theorists say little or nothing explicitly about Hohfeld, some of these writers do use Hohfeldian categories, particularly that of the claim right, in their discussions. Two writers, whose theories of human rights do take the Hohfeldian analysis as their starting point, are Carl Wellman and Rowan Cruft.[66] Wellman shows his Hohfeldian credentials at the start.

> First, one should take legal rights as models of all species of rights, including moral rights. Second, one should analyze the content of any human right in terms of Hohfeld's fundamental legal conceptions or their moral analogues. Then, and only then, could one identify the grounds of any human right.[67]

Cruft is equally committed to the Hohfeldian approach when he says, "my central interest in this book is Hohfeldian claim-rights; rights constituted by duties owed to the right-holder, duties whose violation wrongs the right-holder."[68]

These are examples of human rights theorists who do follow Hohfeld and his analysis. There are many other theorists of human rights, however, who do not follow Hohfeld and indeed often make no mention at all, of him or his analysis or his categories of legal conceptions and relations. This is not to say that they do not sometimes *sound* as though they are committed to a Hohfeldian approach, by referring, say, to claim rights but then show that they can just as easily go against or ignore the Hohfeldian scheme. For example, James Nickel says "almost all human rights are or include claim-rights, and such rights identify a party or parties (the addressees of duty bearers) who must act to make available the freedom or benefit identified by the right's scope. Besides claim-rights there are immunity-rights, power-rights, and privileges (see Hohfeld 1964 and Wenar 2005)."[69] This implies that Nickel is happy to include the other three incidents of rights within his analysis of human rights, thus ignoring Hohfeld's stipulation that it is only the claim-right that is properly called a right. Human rights theorists frequently refer to the importance of the notion of liberty in their analysis of human rights and this is one example of Hohfeld's analysis being ignored, because on Hohfeld's account, a liberty or privilege is quite separate from a claim-right and lacks the essential correlative duty of a claim-right. Carl Wellman, on the other hand, eventually takes an anti-Hohfeldian approach but sticks with the Hohfeldian incidents.

> Moral philosophers have typically assumed that all human rights are claim-rights. This would explain how it is that moral human rights imply correlative moral duties upon either other human beings or the state or both. In fact, I probably shared this assumption when I first began to think seriously about human rights. However, I now believe that there are also other kinds of moral human rights including at least liberty-rights and power-rights and even immunity-rights. This means that moral liberties, powers, and perhaps immunities as well as moral claims can constitute the defining core of human rights.[70]

Wellman proceeds to discuss the notion of "protected liberty rights" which underlines his rebellion against Hohfeld. He says "[i]f there really is any such moral human right to liberty, it must be at the very least a protected liberty, a core liberty protected by a moral duty of others not to prevent or hinder one from exercising this liberty."[71]

The question of the relationship of human rights theorists to Hohfeld is, we can see, a rather confused one. While there are some theorists who clearly state their allegiance to the Hohfeldian analysis there are also some who ignore it and others, like Wellman, who start out following Hohfeld's scheme but end up playing with its categories and stipulations in a somewhat cavalier way.

NOTES

1. Leif Wenar, "Rights." *Stanford Encyclopedia of Philosophy* (Spring 2021 Edition), Edward N. Zalta (ed.), https://plato.stanford.edu/archives/spr2021/entries/rights/.

2. See, for example, Matthew H. Kramer and Hillel Steiner, "Theories of Rights: Is there a Third Way?," *Oxford Journal of Legal Studies* 27, no. 2 (2007): 281–310.

3. See, for example, Rowan Cruft, "The Circularity of the Interest and Will Theories of Rights," in *New Essays on the Nature of Rights*, ed. Mark McBride (Oxford: Hart Publishing, 2017).

4. "*Definition*: 'X has a right' if and only if X can have rights, and, other things being equal, an aspect of X's well-being (his interest) is a sufficient reason for holding some other person(s) to be under a duty." Joseph Raz, *The Morality of Freedom* (Oxford: Oxford University Press, 1986), 166.

5. Gopal Sreenivasan, "A Hybrid Theory of Claim-Rights," *Oxford Journal of Legal Studies* 25, no. 2 (2005): 257–274.

6. Leif Wenar, "The Nature of Claim-Rights," *Ethics* 123, no. 2 (2013): 202–229.

7. Mark McBride, "The Tracking Theory of Rights," in *New Essays on the Nature of Rights*, ed. Mark McBride (Oxford: Hart Publishing, 2017).

8. "Consider a Simple Hybrid model of claim-rights. (SH) Suppose X has a duty to ϕ. Y has a claim-right against X that X ϕ just in case: either Y has the power to waive X's duty to ϕ or Y has no power to waive X's duty to ϕ, but (that is because) Y's disability advances Y's interests on balance." Sreenivasan, "A Hybrid Theory of Claim-Rights," 267.

9. Leif Wenar, "The Nature of Claim-Rights," Ethics, 2, 2013, 202–229.

10. Leif Wenar, "The Nature of Claim-Rights," 218.

11. Leif Wenar, "The Nature of Claim-Rights," 219.

12. Matthew Kramer, N.E. Simmonds and Hillel Steiner, *A Debate Over Rights* (Oxford: Oxford University Press, 1998), 2.

13. Leif Wenar, "Rights."

14. As Maurice Cranston puts it after listing the different types of legal and moral rights. "The place which human rights occupy in my classification is readily understood. Human rights are a form of moral right, and they differ from other moral rights in being the rights of all people at all times and in all situations." Maurice Cranston, *What Are Human Rights?* (New York: Taplinger Publishing Co., Inc., 1973), 21.

15. "In addressing the question of the nature of human rights, an intuitive move has been to turn to the notion of natural rights, whose main formulation can be found in the writings of Grotius, Pufendorf, and Locke." Rowan Cruft, Matthew Liao, and Massimo Renzo eds., *Philosophical Foundations of Human Rights* (Oxford: Oxford University Press, 2015), 4.

16. Preamble of the charter of the United Nations as quoted in Carl Wellman, *The Moral Dimensions of Human Rights*, (New York: Oxford University Press Inc., 2011), 5.

17. Wellman, *The Moral Dimensions of Human Rights*, 5.

18. Jeremy Bentham being the foremost positivist critic of natural rights.

19. David Hume, *A Treatise of Human Nature* (Oxford: Oxford University Press. 1978).

20. James Nickel, *Making Sense of Human Rights* (Berkley and Los Angeles: University of California Press, 1987), Maurice Cranston, *What are Human Rights?* (New York: Taplinger Publishing Co., Inc., 1973), Joel Feinberg, *Social Philosophy*

(New Jersey: Prentice-Hall Inc., 1973), Alan Gewirth, *Human Rights: Essays on Justification and Application* (Chicago: University of Chicago Press, 1982), Jack Donelly, *Universal Human Rights in Theory and Practice* (Ithica, NY: Cornell University Press, 1989).

21. James Nickel, *Making Sense of Human Rights*, John Rawls, *The Law of Peoples* (Cambridge MA: Harvard University Press, 1999), Charles Beitz, *The Idea of Human Rights* (Oxford: Oxford University Press, 2009).

22. James Griffin, *On Human Rights* (Oxford: Oxford University Press, 2008), Jeremy Waldron, "Human Rights: A Critique of the Raz/Rawls Approach," in *Human Rights: Moral or Political?* ed. A. Etinson (Oxford: Oxford University Press, 2018).

23. John Rawls, *The Law of Peoples*, Martha Nussbaum, *Creating Capabilities: The Human Development Approach* (Cambridge, MA: The Belknap Press of Harvard University Press, 2011).

24. Nussbaum could be said to combine needs and well-being with elements of agency and the conception of a good life, bound together under the notion that social justice requires securing certain "capabilities" that are necessary for a life worthy of human dignity. Nussbaum, *Creating Capabilities*.

25. See for example Cranston, *What Are Human Rights?*, 68–69, "To speak of a universal right is to speak of a universal duty. . . . Indeed, if this universal duty were not imposed, what sense could be made of the concept of a universal right?"

26. "Because only a being capable of moral action could possess a moral right, neonates and the irreversibly comatose are incapable of holding any moral human right." Wellman, *The Moral Dimension of Human Rights*, 27.

27. Sumner, *The Moral Foundation of Rights*, vii.

28. *"Act in such a way that you always treat humanity, whether in your own person or in the person of any other, never simply as a means, but always at the same time as an end."* Immanuel Kant, *Groundwork of the Metaphysics of Morals*, trans. H. J. Paton (New York: Harper and Row Publishers, 1964), 96.

29. John Rawls, *The Law of Peoples*, T. M. Scanlon, "Rights, Goals and Fairness," in *Theories of Rights*, ed. Jeremy Waldron (Oxford: Oxford University Press, 1984).

30. Griffin, *On Human Rights*, 33.

31. Griffin, *On Human Rights*, 32.

32. Griffin, *On Human Rights*, 33.

33. Griffin, *On Human Rights*, 152.

34. Griffin, *On Human Rights*, 2.

35. Griffin, *On Human Rights*, 149.

36. Alan Gewirth, *Human Rights: Essays on Justification and Application* (Chicago: University of Chicago Press, 1982).

37. John Tasioulas, "On the Foundations of Human Rights," in *Philosophical Foundations of Human Rights*, eds. Rowan Cruft, Matthew Liao, and Massimo Renzo (Oxford: Oxford University Press, 2015), 50.

38. Tasioulas, "On the Foundations of Human Rights," 50.

39. Tasioulas, "On the Foundations of Human Rights," 55.

40. Tasioulas, "On the Foundations of Human Rights," 70.

41. Massimo Renzo, "Human Needs, Human Rights," in *Philosophical Foundations of Human Rights*, eds. Rowan Cruft, Matthew Liao, and Massimo Renzo (Oxford: Oxford University Press, 2015), 575.

42. Renzo, "Human Needs, Human Rights," 576.

43. Renzo, "Human Needs, Human Rights," 577.

44. Renzo, "Human Needs, Human Rights," 577.

45. Renzo, "Human Needs, Human Rights," 577–578.

46. Renzo, "Human Needs, Human Rights," 582.

47. Renzo, "Human Needs, Human Rights," 582.

48. Renzo, "Human Needs, Human Rights," 583.

49. Renzo, "Human Needs, Human Rights," 587.

50. James Nickel, *Making Sense of Human Rights* (University of Chicago Press, 1987; Malden, MA: Blackwell Publishing, 2007), 53. Citations refer to the Blackwell edition.

51. Mathew Liao, "Human Rights as Fundamental Conditions for a Good Life," in *Philosophical Foundations of Human Rights*, eds. Rowan Cruft, Matthew Liao, and Massimo Renzo (Oxford: Oxford University Press, 2015).

52. Liao, "Human Rights as Fundamental Conditions for a Good Life," 81.

53. Liao, "Human Rights as Fundamental Conditions for a Good Life," 81.

54. Liao, "Human Rights as Fundamental Conditions for a Good Life," 82.

55. Liao, "Human Rights as Fundamental Conditions for a Good Life," 82.

56. Liao, Human Rights as Fundamental Conditions for a Good Life," 82.

57. Liao, Human Rights as Fundamental Conditions for a Good Life," 82.

58. Liao, Human Rights as Fundamental Conditions for a Good Life," 83.

59. Griffin, *On Human Rights*, 32–33.

60. Griffin, *On Human Rights*, 37.

61. Griffin, *On Human Rights*, 38.

62. Griffin, *On Human Rights*, 39.

63. Griffin, *On Human Rights*, 39.

64. Renzo, "Human Needs, Human Rights," 582.

65. Nickel, *Making Sense of Human Rights*, 53.

66. Rowan Cruft, *Human Rights, Ownership, and the Individual* (Oxford: Oxford University Press, 2019), Wellman, *The Moral Dimensions of Human Rights*.

67. Wellman, *The Moral Dimensions of Human Rights*, v.

68. Cruft, *Human Rights, Ownership and the Individual*, 5.

69. Nickel, *Making Sense of Human Rights*, 23.

70. Wellman, *The Moral Dimensions of Human Rights*, 41–42.

71. Wellman, *The Moral Dimensions of Human Rights*, 44.

Chapter 8

Thoughts for Future Rights Theorising

THE CURRENT STATE OF PLAY

The will and interest theories continue to be the most discussed theories of rights despite the persistence of counterexamples and objections to both theories. How might the impasse between the two theories be resolved? In this final chapter, I offer some thoughts on how rights theorising might move forward.

If one broadens the idea of what rights are, or which human characteristics they are a response to, then perhaps it is possible to formulate a view of rights that is more catholic (small c) and less constricting. The majority of counterexamples offered in objection to the two theories are cases where "rights," as commonly understood, are excluded from the theory under examination. There are also, of course, cases where the theory is too generous in its inclusion of such things as the "right to be punished" that does not conform to everyday understanding of what a right it. These are far fewer, however.

Both Hart, for will theory, and Bentham, for interest theory, recognized that their theories do not cover all rights but rejected the idea of what Hart terms "some general formula" that would include more than one way of characterising rights, "I fear that, behind the comfortable appearance of generality, we would have only an unilluminating combination or mere juxtaposition of the choice theory together with the benefit theory; and this would fail to be sensitive to the important reasons for describing only some legally secured benefits, only in some contexts, as legal rights."[1] This sounds like a criticism of current hybrid theory. And yet, the current situation is also unsatisfactory, particularly, in my view, for the will theory, because of the many rights and right-holders that must be left out if we adopt it. I will attempt, in the rest of this chapter, to sketch some ideas for a way forward for rights theory that will resolve some of the issues I have outlined in the last few chapters.

PRELIMINARY THOUGHTS FOR A NEW WAY OF THEORISING INDIVIDUAL RIGHTS

Before the emergence of the notion of a *subjective right* in the late medieval period, what we would now call legal rights and duties were discussed in terms of the privileges accorded to certain individuals or groups due to their legal status and the correlative duties owed by others to those individuals or groups. Even to say this is to misunderstand or mislead, in Tierney's view (following Villey), regarding the radically different way that the word *ius* was used in ancient Rome, because the legal "rights" I have just referred to were not "rights" in our sense, tied to individuals. They inhered in *things* which had legal attributes. So that a piece of land had rights attached to it which meant a person could do things on it, but those "rights" were attached to the land not to the person.[2] There were also discussions conducted (using the term *ius* again) in terms of what was objectively right or what was due to someone as a matter of justice. (e.g., in the colorful example from Villey that I mentioned previously, that *the right of parricide* was to be put into a sack of vipers and thrown into the Tiber).[3] The important point for this discussion is the stark contrast between older discussions of what we would now call legal rights and the new idea, emerging in the medieval period, of subjective moral rights, attaching to or inhering in each individual.

When the new notion of *subjective rights* was theorized in natural rights theories in the early modern period, it introduced an entirely new way of thinking about rights. This idea, of *natural rights,* came to dominate political discourse and became embedded in liberal theory, despite its rejection at a philosophical level by the new empiricists and positivists, in the eighteenth and nineteenth centuries.[4] One effect of that rejection and particularly of Bentham's insistence that rights exist only in law, was the turn to law and to jurisprudence for commentary and theorising on rights, culminating in the dominance of the Hohfeldian analysis and the will and interest theories of rights. In some sense, one could say that it marked the *return* of philosophical thinking on rights to the ambit of law, where it had always been before and to legal rights rather than moral rights.

It has become standard practice for those who commentate and theorize on rights to refer to both legal rights and moral and political rights in their work, often treating them as the same or very similar. Or, perhaps it is more accurate to say that, particularly when the Hohfeldian analysis is used, rights are seen as having the same meaning or intension even when referring to rights within different systems or frameworks, that is, within a legal system or within a framework of moral or political rules or beliefs.[5] The proliferation of rights that are now the subject matter of rights theorising is quite dizzying and of course the addition of *human rights* since the second half of the twentieth century has only added to the number, variety, and complexity of the rights to be theorized and analysed.

The notion of a right, then, is usually taken to cover multiple kinds of rights that individuals may be said to hold and any attempt to theorize and justify the notion of a right is committed to finding a theory that will justify and explain every kind of right there is. (As is clear from the comments on the will and interest theories above, this often proves to be impossible). An exception to the efforts to cover all kinds of rights, including legal rights, within a theory is the recent flurry of work in the *philosophy of human rights*, which usually confines itself to the study of *human rights* specifically. However, as I have already mentioned, the proliferation of human rights means that these explanations and justifications of rights must also cover many different kinds of rights and must also include *legal* human rights where the rights are protected in law. Whether theorists accept the Hohfeldian definition of a right as a claim with correlative duties or some broader definition, they have the task of explaining and justifying a wide variety of rights with an equally wide variety of implications in terms of the actions or protections required to uphold them. As I have shown in the last chapter, attempts to provide a grounding concept for all *human rights* often leads to a multiplication by the back door, as it were, of grounding concepts, so that one grounding concept becomes several, or has several "requirements." One could argue that an advantage of the Hohfeldian analysis is the fact that it says so little about what a right is, beyond being the correlative of a duty. This means that it can be used to cover almost any kind of right (although one obvious exception, mentioned previously, from Hobbes, are the rights held by Hobbesian subjects, which do not fit into Hohfeldian categories). The drawback, on the other hand, is that in keeping all value and content out of the notion of a claim, it fails to justify it or to explain what a right is beyond being the other side of a duty.

My intention is to re-focus on *individual rights*, that is, on the notion that there are certain moral and political rights that all humans have, simply by virtue of being human. These rights, usually now termed *human rights*, are distinct from and have a different justification from certain sorts of legal rights. I am going to make an argument that we should divide rights into several categories. This will allow different grounding concepts which, I argue, will resolve some of the difficulties that current theories encounter (for example, that the will theory cannot account for the rights of those lacking capacity). It is not a new idea to suggest that rights, particularly *human rights*, can be grouped under different headings, for example, of civil and political rights, and social and economic rights and I take a lot from previous thinking in this regard. Previous suggestions of such distinctions, however, are often put forward in response to the duties and actions required to *uphold* the various rights. For example, some social and economic rights require provisions that many states would not be able to fulfil and so it is argued that they should be treated differently from the sort of fundamental political rights that do not require economically expensive provisions by states. I will be focusing instead on the justifications and explanations of certain categories of rights and arguing that they spring from different human characteristics and are justified by different grounding concepts.

I argue that there are significant differences between, say, the right to make a will and the right not to be tortured. And that there are significant differences between the right of a patient in a persistent vegetative state to be treated humanely and with respect and the right to freedom of movement. In the case of the latter, the rights, I argue, arise from different aspects of human nature. The right of a starving refugee to food and shelter and protection does not arise directly from that aspect of human nature that enables humans to act autonomously and freely in the world, rather it arises from that aspect of human nature that always seeks self-preservation and a minimally decent life.

I suggest that rights can be divided into the following four categories:

1. Rights of Assertion
2. Rights of Aspiration
3. Rights of Self-Preservation
4. Rights of (legal/social) Organisation

Rights of Assertion

Rights of Assertion are those rights which we hold as a consequence of that part of our human nature that enables us to assert ourselves and to make claims to such rights. It is that part of our human nature that allows us to act in the world and to make decisions; in other words, to act autonomously and freely. And because we are, by our nature, beings who act freely and autonomously, it is appropriate that we should have rights to whatever is required for us to be able to act freely and autonomously in the world. Autonomy, as Gerald Dworkin demonstrates,[6] is not absolute. None of us is completely free of influences when we act but we can claim practical autonomy when we are not controlled by those influences. Similarly, liberty is not absolute. We need enough liberty to live as free people, not liberty to anything we desire. As Hobbes notes, we cannot live in peace together if we have "a right (liberty) to every thing." A person must be willing, "when others are so too" . . . to "lay down this right to all things; and be contented with so much liberty against other men, as he would allow other men against himself."[7] In other words, as we would now say, we should be free so long as we are not violating the rights of others. Precisely how much liberty we need to live as free or free enough to live a fully human life is open to debate.

Rights of Assertion include those fundamental moral and political rights that are often grouped together as civil and political rights and many are already present in the natural rights documents of the French and American revolutions as well as in the United Nations Declaration of Human Rights, Articles 1–21. Rights such as the right to life, liberty and security of person (Art. 3), the right not to be held in slavery or servitude (4), the right not to be tortured (Art. 5), the right to freedom of movement (Art. 13). And all the rights relating to the principles of the rule of law that protect individuals. In the French Declaration of the Rights of Man, we have the rights to liberty, property, security. and resistance to oppression (Art. 2).

There is much one could say about the notion of liberty and what is meant by it but there is not the space here to have a full discussion of this crucial notion. Hobbes was right to recognize its centrality to the notion of a right, but wrong to restrict it to *freedom from interference* or what has become known as *negative liberty*.[8] Modern lists of human rights include many *positive liberties,* rights to the things we need or *freedom to* rather than *freedom from*. I would also suggest that any modern account of rights must include in its notion of liberty, something close to *republican liberty*—the re-working of the ancient notion of liberty as *freedom from domination* that has been influential in recent political philosophy thanks to the work of writers such as Quentin Skinner[9] and Philip Pettit.[10] This idea, that to be free and autonomous one must also be free of forms of control or restriction that may not be physical, and linked to the notion of being free from arbitrary power, has particular resonance in the light of recent developments in awareness and (in some jurisdictions) in the criminal law, concerning notions such as "coercive control."

Rights of Assertion are generated by that aspect of our human nature that is capable of autonomous and free action. Even those who are currently *less capable* or *incapable* of autonomous and free action, still have rights of assertion. This is reflected in the law that, for example, allows people with dementia to vote, even if they require some help, say to get to the polling station on the correct day. Any living being with the status of human is *potentially* a free, autonomous being. A baby or young child will try to assert their autonomy and liberty before they are capable of either and will gradually become more capable of both. An elderly patient with dementia will be increasingly *unable* to assert autonomy and liberty and yet can be helped to make what autonomous decisions they are capable of. As soon as a patient in a persistent vegetative state wakes up, as some do, she has a right to autonomous, free action. Or, if she is conscious but has "locked-in syndrome" then, if she can communicate her wishes to the doctors, those wishes should be acted upon if reasonable and possible. When someone is completely incapable of any autonomous or free actions then some rights of assertion may be temporarily suspended but their well-being will then be protected by rights of self-preservation, unless and until they are capable of free and autonomous action again.

All the rights we need in order to live freely and autonomously can be included as rights of assertion. Rights of assertion usually give rise to the duties of others, including states, to refrain from interfering with the liberties of individuals and to provide the legal and political provisions and safeguards that are required to uphold the rights.

Rights of Aspiration

Human beings are creatures of aspiration and potential. They have a capacity for creativity, for acquiring knowledge and for exploration and discovery. They are forward looking and capable of making plans for the future. They have abilities and talents that require opportunities and resources in order to be realized and developed. Rights of aspiration are rights to what is needed if we are to live developed and fulfilling lives; to live fully human lives.

Rights of aspiration include such rights as the right "to the pursuit of happiness" of the American Declaration of Independence, the right to education, the right to participate in the arts, to pursue knowledge, to develop talents, to pursue interests and beliefs including religious beliefs. They usually give rise to duties on the part of states and others to provide the necessary resources and not to interfere with or prevent access to those resources. Rights of assertion can be said to be positive liberties (freedom to) rather than negative liberties (freedom from)[11] although they can require rights of non-interference as well as resources to prevent restriction of access.

Rights of Self-Preservation and Well-Being

Rights of self-preservation are the rights of all individuals to be able to live at least to a level allowing a minimally decent life and self-respect. These rights apply particularly to the vulnerable, disadvantaged, and incapacitated. Human beings have certain basic needs that they cannot always fulfil themselves. Resources and help are sometimes required for people to live, and to live a minimally decent life. The most fundamental aspect of human nature is that humans are living beings and strive to preserve themselves. There are rights to whatever is required for each person to live a basically decent life. When persons cannot provide for their own self-preservation, they have a right to assistance. Rights of self-preservation give rise to the duties of others, including states, to provide that assistance. These rights can also be defined as positive liberties. They are "freedoms" in that the upholding of these rights means people are *free to* in the sense of *able to* preserve themselves and to live a minimally decent life. They could also be characterized as "passive rights" in the sense that they require the assistance of others rather than the exercise of power or choice.[12]

If the aspect of human nature that generates these rights is that humans are living beings who strive to preserve themselves then the question arises as to whether other living beings can also generate rights. This is a question that can be put off until a more detailed exploration is possible.

Rights of Legal or Social Organisation

These rights are rights that enable the smooth running or organisation of human affairs, many of which are rights within a legal system. They are distinct from the other three categories in that they are not universal moral rights and are not bestowed simply by virtue of the humanity of the right holder. Rather, they are attached to particular individuals or groups or entities, by virtue of their legal or social status. These rights do not form part of the theory of individual rights as they do not conform to the definition of individual rights as moral and political rights held by all individuals simply by virtue of their humanity. Those that are legal rights can be analysed within the Hohfeldian scheme.

There are many legal rights that do not come into this category; rights not to be killed or assaulted, for example, which exist in criminal law, can be defined as individual rights that are protected in law. Similarly, there are many other *human rights,* which are protected in domestic or international law, so becoming legal rights, but which again, do not come into this category.

THE JUSTIFICATION OF INDIVIDUAL RIGHTS

I argue that there is one overarching moral premise required before we can start to justify individual rights and that is the premise of the equal moral worth of all human beings or persons. Each person has equal, ultimate moral worth or value.[13] The principle of the equality of all humans is also required and taken for granted now, though it was of course new and highly controversial when the early natural rights theories were being developed. This is a necessary baseline without which it is not possible to get a theory of universal moral and political rights going. I hope that it is possible to remain neutral or ecumenical when it comes to the question of which moral theory or theories might support this principle, in other words, to leave open the possibility that it can be reached via different moral theories (or even theologies). This will allow the avoidance of a need to restrict myself to one particular moral theory in order to support this justification of rights. While it may seem that an obvious contender for establishing the equal moral worth of all persons would be some kind of Kantian deontology, it is also the case that for example, Sumner provides a justification of moral rights via consequentialist theory.[14]

The Concept of an Individual Right

The next part of the argument concerns the concept of a right and what it is. I suggest that a right is a *justified claim*. This is in contrast to a *Hohfeldian claim*, which defines a legal relation and has no content over and above the duty it is correlated with and the "no-right" it is opposed to. What I mean by a *justified claim*, on the other hand, is a claim in the sense of "staking a claim," that is, of declaring "this is mine" or "this should be mine." This is a specific use of the term and not perhaps the more general use referred to by Feinberg when he rejects the notion of a "justified claim" as too broad.[15] In this case, I argue, I can claim something as my right if it is required by my nature. If my (human) nature requires it, I can stake a claim to it. It is important to note that the nature referred to is human nature in general not any specific individual's nature. Many other theories of rights appeal to an *aspect* of human nature, often arguing that because human beings are unique in having a particular aspect to their nature (such as agency or "personhood" in Griffin's argument, for example), they therefore have rights.[16] The *justified claims* (rights), I am suggesting, also give rise to duties on the part of others and/or the state. It should be noted that the rights generate or give reasons for the duties, rather than the rights and duties being strictly correlated as in the Hohfeldian system, where it can be said just as well that the duties give rise to the rights as that the rights give rise to the duties.

My view of the relationship of rights to duties is close to that of Joseph Raz and Neil MacCormick in their respective versions of the interest theory, rather than the strict correlativity of Hohfeld. The rights exist first and can exist even before or without the duties they give rise to.[17] Raz defines a right in the following way, " 'X has a right' if and only if X can have rights, and, other things being equal, an aspect of X's well-being (his interest) is a sufficient reason for holding some other person(s) to be under a duty."[18]

If a person found herself alone in the world after a terrible plague had killed everyone else, she would still have a right to live as a (fully) human being. She could still "stake her claim" to her human life as something she should have.[19] While it is a strongly intuitive notion that we have rights only in relation to the protections given by other people, if the rights are (as I argue) generated by the requirements of human nature (given the equal, ultimate moral worth of all human beings), then, in theory, they would apply even if there was only one person left in the world. What the rights would not do, in such a situation, is give rise to protections, except perhaps in some psychological sense or in the sense of giving rise to duties to oneself.

Human Nature—The Kind of Beings Humans Are

Human beings are first and foremost living beings and further, living beings of the animal kind. As living animals, an important part of their nature is to act to preserve themselves. They are also living beings who are capable of autonomous action; humans contemplate and make choices informed by desires and beliefs, as independent individuals. Beyond this, they are also capable of creativity, of acquiring and exploring knowledge, of discovery, of spirituality and of morality. I argue that it is this *multiple nature* that makes us human, rather than any one trait that provides the unique ingredient. Theorists often pick one facet of human nature such as rationality or agency or sentience; and make the case that it is this one special thing that makes us human. Griffin refers to this as our "distinctively *human* existence" and this special status "centres on our being agents—deliberating, assessing, choosing, and acting to make what we see as a good life for ourselves." So, for Griffin, it is agency that gives us our "human standing" and human rights "can then be seen as protections of our human standing."[20] An older tradition picks out rationality as the unique ingredient, and the one that separates us from the other animals (often together with some theological premises such as being made in God's image and having a soul). This enabled arguments that gave humans a special moral status. That special status is harder to establish today with the loss of ubiquitous religious belief and increasing scientific work on animal intelligence and sentience.

It is our nature to live and it is our nature to live a specifically human life, including the necessities for physical health and well-being. It is our nature to live as autonomous, free individuals who may make decisions and choices, develop our talents and abilities and pursue goals, for a certain kind of life, enjoy certain activities and achievements. It is our nature to have close relationships with others and to pursue happiness and fulfilment.

The Moral Aspect to Duties Upholding Rights

The Hohfeldian approach to rights emphasizes the correlative duties that are inextricably attached to rights and this can lead to a view that duties are assigned to individuals without their active participation. Just as laws are passed without our direct involvement that then assign legal duties and prohibitions to us that we are obliged to obey, so the duties correlative to rights can seem to be assigned to individuals without their active participation. In the case of human rights and other rights that are protected in law this is of course quite appropriate, that individuals are obliged to obey the law. But there is another aspect to the duties that individual rights give rise to and that is the *active moral* aspect of those duties. When a person acknowledges the right of another, she takes on duties not to violate that right and where necessary, to uphold it. This is clear in the discourse on rights that is now prevalent in most societies.

I have already referred to the moral premise that is required before moral rights can be justified—that of the equal and ultimate moral worth or value of all human beings—and this premise leads easily to the Rawlsian principle of equal respect for all persons. If individuals also have rights, then all other persons have moral duties to respect those rights. Carl Wellman says the following about the special moral status of human beings in relation to human rights.

> Normal adult human beings differ from all the other beings known to us in a way that commands our respect. There is something about human nature, often called human dignity, that confers upon human beings a very special moral status.[21]

This "special moral status" means that the notion of people having rights, coming from that status, has particular moral importance. What is sometimes missing from accounts of individual rights is a recognition of the influence of the moral aspect of duties to respect and protect rights. The weight that the notion of rights, particularly of *human rights*, now carries in political and moral discourse, can, in part, be attributed to this moral response. I argue that the rights for which this moral response is most apparent are rights of self-preservation. When some human beings are in dire need or distress, it excites a strong moral response in others. This means that if a duty, legal or moral, to help, is assigned, it is bolstered by the moral response which the need or distress engenders. In light of this response, we could say that rights of self-preservation are also rights of compassion. This moral response also explains, in my view, why the question arises as to the possibility that other animals, particularly those we know to experience pain and suffering and some level of awareness, should be included within rights discourse. One traditional objection to this idea is that other animals are not capable of acting on duties to uphold the rights of others. But it is also the case that babies and those in persistent vegetative states are equally incapable of acting on duties to others. The muscular notion that rights are only appropriate for those strong enough to bear responsibilities, fails to recognise that aspect of the moral response to need and pain that requires no "pay back."

RIGHTS

The first and most fundamental right is the right to live as a (fully) human being.

This right is justified by:

1. Human beings have equal and ultimate moral status. They are thus worthy of respect and moral recognition and action.
2. It is the nature of a human being to live as a (fully) human being.
3. Each individual human being can stake a claim to what is theirs by nature. These claims provide reasons for imposing duties on others, including states.
4. Each human being can stake a claim to live as a fully human being
5. Each individual human being has a right to live as a (fully) human being.

From the fundamental right to live as a (fully) human being we can derive all the other rights within the first three categories: rights of assertion, rights of aspiration and rights of self-preservation. These three categories together cover what are often termed "human rights," but I will avoid that term as it also has implications regarding complex legal provisions in both international and domestic law and I wish to restrict my comments to moral and political rights. I will therefore stick to the term "individual rights." The fourth category of *rights of legal and social organisation* is there for the purposes of exclusion. It is my intention to exclude these sorts of technical legal rights and customary social rights from theorising about individual rights. It has been a tendency in rights theorising, since the turn to jurisprudence after the discrediting of natural rights theorising, to include legal rights and indeed to often take legal rights as the paradigm case of rights.

Rights of Assertion are generated by that aspect of our human nature that is capable of autonomous and free action. Even those who are currently *incapable* of autonomous and free action have the right to it as human beings. As long as they have the status of human, they are *potentially* free, autonomous beings. As soon as a patient in a persistent vegetative state wakes up, as some do, she has a right to autonomous free action.

Rights of Aspiration also arise from our capability for autonomous and free action with the addition of our extra capacity for creativity, knowledge and exploration. Rights of Self-Preservation arise from that part of human nature that requires certain basic needs to be met for health, well-being and self-respect, and at bottom, for survival.

CONCLUDING THOUGHTS

The tentative thoughts set out in this chapter are an attempt to find new ways of tackling some of the issues in rights theorising that I have raised in previous chapters. Many of these thoughts are not new by any means but perhaps just put together in slightly different ways, in order to avoid some of the problems I have outlined throughout the book. At best, this chapter provides a starting point for the further development and refinement of the ideas that are sketched so briefly here. Whether or not my own first efforts at tinkering with rights theory bear any fruit, I hope I have succeeded in drawing attention to some issues both with the way that the history of rights theory has been written and with recent and current approaches to rights theory, and particularly with the widely adopted Hohfeldian approach to rights.

NOTES

1. H. L. A. Hart, "Legal Rights," in *Essays on Bentham: Jurisprudence and Political Theory*, ed. H. L .A. Hart (Oxford: Oxford University Press, 1982), 193.

2. Brian Tierney, *The Idea of Natural Rights* (Atlanta, GA: Scholars Press, Emory University, 1997), 16.

3. Tierney, *The Idea of Natural Rights*, 16.

4. See chapter 2.

5. See, for example, Joel Feinberg, *Social Philosophy* (Englewood Cliffs, NJ: Prentice-Hall Inc., 1973), 67. "A man has a legal right when the official recognition of his claim (as valid) is called for by the governing rules. This definition, of course, hardly applies to moral rights, but that is not because the genus of which moral rights are a species is something other than claims. A man has a moral right when he has a claim, the recognition of which is called for—not (necessarily) by legal rules—but by moral principles, or the principles of an enlightened conscience."

6. Gerald Dworkin, *The Theory and Practice of Autonomy* (Cambridge: Cambridge University Press, 1988).

7. Hobbes, *Leviathan*, [1651], ed., N. Malcolm 2012, Vol. 2, Ch. 14, 200.

8. Isaiah Berlin, *Four Essays on Liberty* (Oxford: Oxford University Press, 1969).

9. See Quentin Skinner, *Liberty before Liberalism* (Cambridge: Cambridge University Press, 1998) and *Hobbes and Republican Liberty* (Cambridge: Cambridge University Press, 2008).

10. See Philip Pettit, *Republicanism: A Theory of Freedom and Government* (Oxford: Oxford University Press, 1997) and Cecile Laborde and John Maynor eds., *Republicanism and Political Theory* (Oxford: Blackwell Publishing, 2008).

11. Isaiah Berlin, *Four Essays on Liberty* (Oxford: Oxford University Press, 1969).

12. See chapter 1 for the distinction between active and passive rights.

13. The principle of the equality of all humans is also required and taken for granted now, though it was of course new and highly controversial when the early natural rights theories were being developed.

14. L. W. Sumner, *The Moral Foundation of Rights* (New York: Oxford University Press, 1987).

15. "I prefer to define rights as valid claims rather than justified ones, because I suspect that justification is too broad a qualification." Joel Feinberg, *Social Philosophy* (Englewood Cliffs NJ: Prentice-Hall Inc., 1973), 67.

16. "In what should we say human rights are grounded? Well, primarily in personhood. Out of the notion of personhood we can generate most of the list of conventional human rights." James Griffin, *On Human Rights* (Oxford: Oxford University Press, 2008), 33.

17. On the right of children to care and nurture MacCormick says "I will aver that it is *because* children have that right that it is good that legal provision should be made in the first instance . . . and secondarily to provide for its performance by alternative foster parents. . . . So far from its being the case that the remedial provision is constitutive of the right, the fact is rather that recognition of the right justifies the imposition of the remedial provision." D. N. MacCormick, "Rights in Legislation," in *Law, Morality and Society, Essays in Honour of H. L. A. Hart*, eds. P. M. S. Hacker and J. Raz (Oxford: Oxford University Press, 1977) (quoting from a conference paper entitled "Children's Rights" presented to the Association of Legal and Social Philosophy, April 1975).

18. Joseph Raz, *The Morality of Freedom* (Oxford: Oxford University Press, 1986), 166.

19. My thanks to a member of my Morality and Law class at Kent Law School, 2019, for pushing me to think more about the seemingly reasonable assertion that rights can only exist in a social context. While it is strongly intuitive that we have rights only in relation to other people, if the rights are (as I argue) prior to the duties they justify imposing on others, then they exist even without a possibility of those duties being imposed.

20. James Griffin, *On Human Rights*, 32–33.

21. Carl Wellman, *The Moral Dimensions of Human Rights* (New York: Oxford University Press, 2011), 21.

Bibliography

The American Declaration of Independence, 1776. https://www.archives.gov/founding-docs/declaration-transcript.

Beitz, Charles. *The Idea of Human Rights*. Oxford: Oxford University Press, 2009.

Berlin, Isaiah. *Four Essays on Liberty*. Oxford: Oxford University Press, 1969.

Bentham, Jeremy. "Anarchical Fallacies." (1796) In *The Works of Jeremy Bentham*, edited by John Bowring. Edinburgh: William Tait, 1843.

———. "Supply without Burthern." (1793) London: J. Debrett, 1795.

Bix, Brian. *Jurisprudence: Theory and Context*. London: Sweet and Maxwell, 2006.

Cranston, Maurice. *What Are Human Rights?* New York: Taplinger Publishing Co., Inc., 1973.

Cruft, Rowan S., Mathew Liao, and Massimo Renzo. *Philosophical Foundations of Human Rights*. Oxford: Oxford University Press, 2015.

Cruft, Rowan. "The Circularity of the Interest and Will Theories of Rights." In *New Essays on the Nature of Rights*, edited by Mark McBride, 169–186. Oxford: Hart Publishing, 2017.

Curran, Eleanor. "Can Rights Curb the Hobbesian Sovereign? The Full Right to Self-Preservation, Duties of Sovereignty and the Limitations of Hohfeld." *Law and Philosophy* 25 (2006): 243–265.

———. *Reclaiming the Rights of the Hobbesian Subject*. Basingstoke: Palgrave Macmillan, 2007.

d'Entreves, A. P. *Natural Law, An Introduction to Legal Philosophy*. London: Hutchinson and Co., 1951.

Digges, Dudley. *The Unlawfulness of Subjects Taking up Arms Against the Sovereign*. London, 1644.

Dow, F. D. *Radicalism in the English Revolution 1640-1660*. Oxford: Basil Blackwell, 1985.

Donelly, Jack. *Universal Human Rights in Theory and Practice*, 1st ed. Ithaca, NY: Cornell University Press, 1989.

Dunn, John. *The Political Thought of John Locke: An Historical Account of the 'Two Treatises of Government'*. Cambridge: Cambridge University Press, 1969.

Feinberg, Joel. *Social Philosophy*. Englewood Cliffs NJ: Prentice-Hall Inc., 1973.

Finkelstein, Claire. "A Puzzle About Hobbes on Self-Defence." *Pacific Philosophical Quarterly* 82, nos. 3–4 (2001): 332–361.

Finnis, John. *Natural Law and Natural Rights*. Oxford: Oxford University Press, 1980.

Freeman, M. D. A. *Lloyd's Introduction to Jurisprudence*, 8th ed. London: Sweet and Maxwell, 2008.

French Declaration of the Rights of Man, 1789.

Gauthier, David. *The Logic of Leviathan*. Oxford: Clarendon Press, 1969.

Gewirth, Alan. *Human Rights: Essays on Justification and Application*. Chicago: University of Chicago Press, 1982.

Griffin, James. *On Human Rights*. Oxford: Oxford University Press, 2008.

Grotius, Hugo. *The Rights of War and Peace (De Iure Belli ac Pacis)*. 1625. Washington and London: M. Walter Dunne 1901; facsimile published by Adamant Media: Boston, 2005.

Hampton, Jean. *Hobbes and the Social Contract Tradition*. Cambridge: Cambridge University Press, 1986.

Harris, J. W. *Legal Philosophies*. 2nd ed. London: Butterworths, 1997.

Hart, H. L. A. *Essays on Bentham: Jurisprudence and Political Theory*. Oxford: Oxford University Press, 1982.

———. "Are There Any Natural Rights." In *Theories of Rights*, edited by Jeremy Waldron, 77–90. Oxford: Oxford University Press, 1984.

———. "Legal Rights." In *Essays on Bentham: Jurisprudence and Political Theory*, edited by H. L. A. Hart, 163–163. Oxford: Oxford University Press, 1982.

Hobbes, Thomas. *Leviathan*. 1651. Edited by C. B. Macpherson. London: Penguin Classics, 1982.

———. *Leviathan*. 1651. Edited by C. B. Macpherson. London: Penguin Books, 1968.

———. *Leviathan*. 1651. Edited by N. Malcolm, Vol. 2. Oxford: Oxford University Press, 2012.

———. *On the Citizen*. 1647. Edited by Richard Tuck and Michael Silverthorne. Cambridge: Cambridge University Press, 1998

———. "The Elements of Law." In *Human Nature and De Corpore Politico*, edited by J. C. A. Gaskin. Oxford: Oxford University Press, 1994.

Hohfeld, Wesley. *Fundamental Legal Conceptions as Applied in Judicial Reasoning*. New Haven: Yale University Press, 1919.

Hooker, Richard. Of the Lawes of Ecclesiastical Polity. 1594. London: Andrew Crooke, 1666.

Hume, David. *A Treatise of Human Nature*. 1739. Edited by Ernest C. Mossner. London: Penguin Books, 1969.

———. *A Treatise of Human Nature*, 2nd ed. Oxford: Oxford University Press. 1978.

Kant, Immanuel. *Groundwork of the Metaphysics of Morals*. Translated by H. J. Paton. New York: Harper and Row Publishers, 1964.

Kavka, Gregory. *Hobbesian Moral and Political Theory.* Princeton: Princeton University Press, 1986.

Kramer, Mathew, N. E. Simmonds, and Hillel Steiner. *A Debate Over Rights.* Oxford: Oxford University Press, 1998.

———. "Rights Without Trimmings." In *A Debate Over Rights,* edited by Matthew Kramer, N. E. Simmonds and Hillel Steiner, 7–111. Oxford: Oxford University Press, 1998.

Kramer, Matthew H., and Hillel Steiner. "Theories of Rights: Is there a Third Way?" *Oxford Journal of Legal Studies* 27, no. 2 (2007): 281–310.

Kymlicka, Will. *Contemporary Political Philosophy.* Oxford: Clarendon Press, 1990.

Laborde, Cecile, and John Maynor eds. *Republicanism and Political Theory.* Oxford: Blackwell Publishing, 2008.

Liao, Mathew. "Human Rights as Fundamental Conditions for a Good Life." In *Philosophical Foundations of Human Rights,* edited by Rowan Cruft, Matthew Liao, and Massimo Renzo, 79–100. Oxford: Oxford University Press, 2015.

Lilburne, John. *The Charters of London, or, the Second Part of Londons Liberty in Chains Discovered.* London: 1646.

Locke, John. *Second Treatise of Government.* 1690. Edited by C. B. Macpherson. Indianapolis: Hackett Publishing Company Inc., 1980.

———. *Two Treatises of Government.* 1690. Edited by Peter Laslett. Cambridge: Cambridge University Press, 1960.

MacCormick, D. N. "Rights in Legislation." In *Law, Morality and Society: Essays in Honour of H. L. A. Hart,* edited by P. Hacker and J. Raz, 189–209. Oxford: Oxford University Press, 1977.

MacDonald, Margaret. "Natural Rights." In *Theories of Rights,* edited by Jeremy Waldron, 21–40. Oxford: Oxford University Press, 1984.

Mackie, J. L. "Can there be a Right-based Moral Theory?" In *Theories of Rights,* edited by Jeremy Waldron, 168–181. Oxford: Oxford University Press, 1984.

McBride, Mark, ed. *New Essays on the Nature of Rights.* Oxford: Hart Publishing Plc, 2017.

McBride, Mark. "The Tracking Theory of Rights." In *New Essays on the Nature of Rights,* edited by Mark McBride, 149–168. Oxford: Hart Publishing, 2017.

Marx, Karl. On the Jewish Question." (1843) *Deutsch-Französische Jahrbücher* (1944). https://www.marxists.org/archive/marx/works/1844/jewish-question/.

Mazzolini da Prierio, Silvestro. *Summa Summarum quae Silvestrina nuncupatur.* Lyons: 1539 (1st ed, Bologna: 1515).

Moore, G. E. *Principia Ethica.* London: Cambridge University Press, 1903.

Murphy, Mark. "The Natural Law Tradition in Ethics." In *Stanford Encyclopedia of Philosophy* (Stanford University 2019). Article first published 23 September 2002; last modified 26 May 2019. https://plato.stanford.edu/entries/natural-law-ethics/.

Murphy, Jeffie G., and Jules L. Coleman. *Philosophy of Law, An Introduction to Jurisprudence.* London: Westview Press, 1990.

Nagel, Thomas. "Hobbes's Concept of Obligation." *The Philosophical Review* 59 (1959): 68–83.

Nickel, James. *Making Sense of Human Rights*, 1st ed. Berkley and Los Angeles: University of California Press, 1987.

Nussbaum, Martha. *Creating Capabilities: The Human Development Approach*. Cambridge, MA: The Belknap Press of Harvard University Press, 2011.

O'Neill, Onora. *Toward Justice and Virtue: A Constructive Account of Practical Reasoning*. Cambridge: Cambridge University Press, 1996.

———. *A Question of Trust*. Cambridge: Cambridge University Press, 2002.

———. "The Dark Side of Human Rights." *International Affairs* 81, no. 2 (2005): 427–439.

———. "Response to John Tasioulas." In *Philosophical Foundations of Human Rights*, edited by Rowan S. Cruft, Mathew Liao and Massimo Renzo, *Philosophical Foundations of Human Rights*. New York: Oxford University Press, 2015.

Placani, Adriana, and Stearns Broadhead. "Right to be Punished." *European Journal of Analytic Philosophy* 16, no. 1 (2004): 53–74.

Pettit, Philip. *Republicanism: A Theory of Freedom and Government*. Oxford: Oxford University Press, 1997.

Rawls, John. *A Theory of Justice*. Cambridge, MA: The Belknap Press of Harvard University Press, 1971.

Raz, Joseph. *The Morality of Freedom*. Oxford: Oxford University Press, 1986.

Renzo, Massimo. "Human Needs, Human Rights." In *Philosophical Foundations of Human Rights*, edited by Rowan Cruft, Matthew Liao, and Massimo Renzo, 571–587. Oxford: Oxford University Press, 2015.

Russell, Paul, and Anders Kraal. "Hume on Religion." In *Stanford Encyclopedia of Philosophy*. Stanford University, 2017. Article first published 4 October, 2005; last modified 27 March 2017. https://plato.stanford.edu/archives/sum2017/entries/hume-religion/.

Ryan, Alan. "Hobbes's Political Philosophy." In *The Cambridge Companion to Hobbes*, edited by Tom Sorell, 208–245. Cambridge: Cambridge University Press, 1996.

Scanlon, T. M. "Rights, Goals and Fairness." In *Theories of Rights*, edited by Jeremy Waldron, 137–152. Oxford: Oxford University Press, 1984.

Simmons, A. J. *The Lockean Theory of Rights*. Princeton: Princeton University Press, 1992.

Skinner, Quentin. *Liberty before Liberalism*. Cambridge: Cambridge University Press, 1998.

———. *Hobbes and Republican Liberty*. Cambridge: Cambridge University Press, 2008.

Sommerville, J. P. ed. *Sir Robert Filmer, Patriarcha and Other Writings*. Cambridge: Cambridge University Press, 1991.

Sreenivasan, Gopal. "A Hybrid Theory of Claim-Rights." *Oxford Journal of Legal Studies* 25, no. 2 (2005): 257–274.

Strauss, Leo. *The Political Philosophy of Hobbes. Its Basis and Its Genesis* (1936). Translated by Elsa M Sinclair. Chicago: University of Chicago Press, 1952 (Midway Reprint 1984).

———. *Natural Right and History*. Chicago: University of Chicago Press, 1950.

Sreedhar, Susanne. *Hobbes on Resistance*. New York: Cambridge University Press, 2010.

Sumner, L. W. *The Moral Foundation of Rights*. Oxford: Oxford University Press, 1984.

Tasioulas, John. "On the Foundations of Human Rights." In *Philosophical Foundations of Human Rights*, edited by Rowan Cruft, Matthew Liao, and Massimo Renzo, 45–70. Oxford: Oxford University Press, 2015).

Taylor, A. E. "The Ethical Doctrine of Hobbes." *Philosophy* 13 (October 1938): 406–424.

Tierney, Brian. "The Idea of Natural Rights-Origins and Persistence." *Northwestern Journal of Human Rights* 2, no. 1 (2004): 2–12.

———. *The Idea of Natural Rights*. Michigan: Eerdmans Publishing Co., 2001. First published 1997 by Scholars Press for Emory University.

———. "Historical Roots of Modern Rights: Before Locke and After." *Ave Maria Law Review* 3, no. 1 (2005): 23–43.

Tuck, Richard. *Natural Rights Theories: Their Origin and Development*. Cambridge: Cambridge University Press, 1979.

Universal Declaration of Human Rights, United Nations General Assembly, Paris December 1948.

Waldron, Jeremy ed. *Theories of Rights*. Oxford: Oxford University Press, 1984.

———, ed. *Liberal Rights: Collected Papers 1981–1991*. Cambridge: Cambridge University Press, 1993.

———. "The Role of Rights in Practical Reasoning: 'Rights' versus 'Needs.'" *The Journal of Ethics*, 4 (2000): 115–135.

——— *God, Locke, and Equality: Christian Foundations in Locke's Political Thought*. Cambridge: Cambridge University Press, 2002.

———. "Human Rights: A Critique of the Raz/Rawls Approach." In *Human Rights: Moral or Political?*, edited by A. Etinson, 118–137. Oxford: Oxford University Press, 2018.

Warrender, Howard. *The Political Philosophy of Hobbes: His Theory of Obligation*. Oxford: Clarendon Press, 1957.

Wellman, Carl. *The Moral Dimensions of Human Rights*. New York: Oxford University Press, 2011.

Wenar, Leif. "Rights." In *The Stanford Encyclopedia of Philosophy* (Stanford University 2005) Article first published 19 December 2005; last modified 2020) https://plato.stanford.edu/archives/spr2021/entries/rights/.

———. "The Nature of Claim-rights." *Ethics*, 123, no. 2 (2013): 202–229.

Index

Note: Page numbers followed by 'n' refer to notes.

About the Author

Eleanor Curran was a senior lecturer at Kent law School, University of Kent, until 2021. She now holds honorary positions with Kent Law School and the Department of Philosophy, University of Kent. She earned her PhD in philosophy from the City University of New York in 1998. Since then she has been a teaching fellow and tutor at King's College London and a 'research philosopher' at The Royal Hospital for Neuro-Disability. She held a lectureship at Keele University Law School and a lectureship and senior lectureship at Kent Law School, University of Kent. In 2007 she published *Reclaiming the Rights of the Hobbesian Subject* (Basingstoke: Palgrave Macmillan, 2007). She primarily publishes work on Hobbes's political thought and theory of rights and its interpretation. She also has publications and conference contributions in Brain Computer Interface (BCI) Systems, Medical Ethics and Legal Ethics.